The Ultimate
Life Skills for Teens

Master Your Essential Health, Time, Relationships, Money, and Decision Management

Confidently Overcome Your Communication, Prioritization, Conflict, Future Planning, and Problem Solving Challenges!

M.J. Sal

Congratulations on taking the step towards learning the ultimate life skills for teens!

I'm honored to go through this journey with you, and as a token of appreciation and further encouragement, I would love to give away 3 gifts to my readers.

You can also type in the address below in your browser.

https://mailchi.mp/36517d071d9b/teens-matter

Get in touch with me for any comments, bonuses, and new book releases:

https://www.facebook.com/groups/teensmatter

https://weww.facebook.com/m.j.salauthor

https://www.instagram.com/m.j.salauthor

m.j.salauthor@gmail.com

from various sources. Please consult a licensed professional before attempting any techniques outlined in this book.

By reading this document, the reader agrees that under no circumstances is the author responsible for any losses, direct or indirect, that are incurred as a result of the use of the information contained within this document, including, but not limited to, errors, omissions, or inaccuracies.

Table of Contents

Introduction

If you were to have met my teenagers about four years ago, you would have thought them to be typical kids—maybe even a little rowdier than your average group of adolescents.

My children are brilliant kids. However, like many teens, they struggled to find who they were and their place in society. They seemed to lack motivation, direction, and purpose. I grew worried as I watched my teen daughter struggle to communicate or understand why she felt so misunderstood by her peers, and my preteen son seemed to have a hard time adjusting to the new family dynamics after a family move. As a result, I was concerned that they would lash out in frustration, as many teens do.

I saw my kids go up and down as their moods, confidence, and self-esteem fluctuated. They often lacked the will to push through anything that felt too difficult or that required mental fortitude and focus. As their mother, their confidant, I felt lost. I wanted to help them—to give them the tools they needed to become productive, and confident members of society. But I didn't know where to start.

That's when I knew that something had to change. As a parent in this situation, I initially thought my kids just needed more structure and tougher guidance. After all, we tend to repeat the parenting strategies we've seen growing up. But one day, I took a breath and looked at them in a new light. I realized my kids needed something more than traditional parenting techniques to help them navigate through the tough teenage years.

What they really needed was something that went beyond just strict rules and discipline. My children needed a significant shift in mindset. They needed a reframing of what it meant to be a teen and the skills to embody this new attitude. That's when I utilized my versatile background in education and health sciences to introduce my kids to the world of personal development. My goal was to provide them with the resources to become independent and successful adults.

When I was a teen myself, I lacked the proper direction. In real-time, I saw how that was also affecting my kids. I didn't know what my purpose was, which caused me to feel like a "goner." Through personal development, however, I discovered I could create the life I wanted and then use this same approach to guide my children. I found that this alternative approach was very well-received by my teens and has been the key to helping them reach their full potential.

Through personal development, I have seen my children become more aware of themselves as individuals, more confident in their interactions, better communicators, and overall happier people. Not only have they become excellent students, but they've also found a passion for sports, music, and art, all of which have provided them with valuable life skills to carry forward into adulthood.

2

It has been an incredibly rewarding journey I am still on today with them.

These years are critical times for development and personal growth. I believe that this development has the power to unlock the greatness in every individual, no matter their age. It has been an invaluable experience for our family and one that I highly recommend to other parents searching for more than traditional methods of parenting.

I have now been helping teens build up their personal development skills for the past few years. I have seen firsthand the amazing results that personal development can bring to individual teens, especially those who feel lost and lack direction in their lives. My goal with each teen I work with is to help them unlock their potential and discover their unique gifts.

The info I'm sharing with you is what I wish I had access to when I was a teenager. If I could do it all over again, knowing what I know today, I would do it differently. That's why I believe this book can be of great use to you and other teens. Between my extensive years of experience with teens and being a parent myself, who have directly been involved with my children's issues and struggles, I will always try to find the best solutions for them on a regular basis.

The book will cover a range of topics, including personal development and goal setting, communication and relationships, emotional intelligence, and mindfulness— skills that I would like to help you achieve. What you're about to learn matters deeply to me because it has helped my own teens and others to cope and resolve their issues better. It brings me immense joy when I see how personal development has transformed my children's lives. They are more confident and open-minded and have learned the skills necessary to pursue their dreams and live fulfilling lives. I feel proud to have been a part of this journey with them, and I am excited for what the future holds.

Through continuous learning, by starting at an early age and going beyond the school curriculum or family and friends' circle, you can have a better vision of the world and, eventually, become successful adults with positive life markers. Taking the time to learn the skills in advance helps tremendously in time when that skill is needed.

Throughout the chapters of this book, we will be introducing two young lads, Bernadette, and Bradley. There were two young children, Bradley, and Bernadette, who were inseparable. From the moment they met in kindergarten, the two children developed an unbreakable bond of friendship. Despite their similarities, each child had unique challenges and experiences that set them apart. They share similar experiences to you and have relatable stories in each of the chapters. But first, here's a quick introduction of our two friends.

Bernadette was an outgoing tomboy who loved astronomy and often felt left out by her female peers. She had trouble fitting in with them. Bernadette was most interested in playing with the boys instead of engaging in traditional girly activities like shopping or gossiping. Bradley was more reserved and found it difficult to make friends due to his shyness. He was also unusual in that he enjoyed more artistic pursuits, such as painting and playing the guitar, rather than playing sports or video games like his classmates.

As they grew older together, the two dealt with different issues, such as bullying and peer pressure, while trying to stay true to themselves. They grew out of some of their tendencies and grew into new ones. They both experienced body changes during puberty, which added another layer of complexity to their relationship as they navigated new feelings and emotions. Bernadette embraced her body transformation at a much faster rate than her friend. But she still shared her newfound understanding of self-love with him until he reached a similar level of confidence for himself.

They leaned on each other for support during these tumultuous years of growing up. Even though they faced unique struggles, neither felt alone nor isolated from one another's experiences. Through it all, their friendship remained strong as ever despite external pressures from those around them who could not comprehend how two people so different could be such close friends. Through shared laughter and tears, they weathered every storm together until eventually graduating high school as best friends, just like when they first met in kindergarten many years ago.

Bernadette and Bradley are here to help you understand that what you're experiencing is normal. The confusion or angst you may feel is completely normal. But we're here to show you how to manage them in easy steps so you can enjoy your teen years, while getting ready and prepared for adulthood.

I encourage you to read through this book at least once.

After that, I invite you to revisit those areas you want to understand better or practice further. Go through exercises and even share them with your best friends to exercise with you. Encourage friends and family members to read this book if you feel the content or exercises can help them as well. Also Help others to find this book by leaving a review, after you're done reading. Let's get started!

Chapter 1:

Hygiene and Grooming

You have most definitely observed your changing body, maybe experiencing the appearance of dandruff, the growth of unwanted hair, acne issues, or strong body odor.

You see, as we get older, our bodies, thoughts, and emotions change. While this is completely normal and even to be expected, it can often be difficult to deal with, as adapting to any change can normally be a mentally depressing and physically a draining task. However, you can choose to do nothing about it and wonder what if or learn a few related skills and add it to your life skills toolbox to give you a hand with these inevitable changes.

This new skill set can continue to serve you well for the rest of your life when you get used to implementing it into your daily routine.

The first important thing you need to learn, in order to stay healthy and happy, is to practice good health habits like hygiene and grooming!

Good hygiene and grooming techniques are great for feeling healthy and refreshed. It will also help you feel confident, cool, and self-assured while socializing with friends or in public. It's almost like you are poised and ready to face the world with every challenge it throws your way by simply feeling great about your appearance and health.

Bernadette and Bradley, two long-time teenage friends, discussed these important topics, one day.

Bernadette started the conversation by asking, "Bradley, how important do you think it is to take care of our hygiene and grooming?"

Bradley replied, "It's very important, Bernadette! Good hygiene routines like washing our hands, taking showers regularly, brushing our teeth, and wearing clean clothes, are crucial for our health and well-being."

Bernadette nodded in agreement and added, "And grooming is also essential to maintain a good appearance and boost self-confidence. It includes things like trimming our nails, brushing our hair, and wearing clean and appropriate clothing."

8

Bradley chuckled, "I remember when we were younger, we didn't care much about these things. But as we've grown older, we've come to realize the importance of good hygiene and grooming. It not only helps us maintain good health but also reflects our personality and how we present ourselves to the world."

Bernadette nodded and said, "Grooming also includes taking care of our skin. It can be as basic as washing our face regularly or using sunscreen to protect ourselves from harmful sun rays. These small habits can lead to significant benefits like preventing acne, dark spots, and even skin cancer."

Bradley nodded in agreement, "Another important aspect of grooming is having a clean shave or well-groomed facial hair. It adds to our overall appearance and gives a neat and tidy look."

Bernadette and Bradley continued discussing their daily grooming and hygiene routines, realizing that these habits not only maintain their appearance but protect their overall health and well-being.

In conclusion, good hygiene and grooming are crucial elements to ensure your health, confidence boost, and presenting yourselves in a positive light.

This chapter will show you how to implement them into your daily routines in a few very easy and efficient steps. So, let's all take the time to learn and incorporate these small habits into our daily routines to maintain optimal health and personal hygiene.

What Is Hygiene?

Hygiene is the practice of keeping the body clean to help stop the spread of germs and other microbes that can cause illness. Good hygiene habits are important for staying healthy, especially during adolescence, when teens are more likely to be active and socialize with their peers.

Hygiene comes in all shapes and sizes and doesn't just include the act of washing your hands. It also includes other practices such as taking regular showers, brushing your teeth twice a day, washing your face daily, and changing into fresh clothes daily.

Practicing good hygiene can go beyond your own body's cleanliness. For instance, hygiene can include keeping all surfaces in your home (especially in bathrooms and kitchens) sanitized regularly by cleaning them with soap and hot water or disinfectant wipes. However, hygiene isn't just about physical cleanliness—it also applies to mental and emotional health, which are as important. Overall, our hygiene can have many components, all of which can affect our physical and emotional health.

What Is Grooming?

In short, grooming is a process of taking care of your physical appearance. Meaning it is very important to also stay neat while having good hygiene. Grooming includes activities like brushing and styling your hair, applying moderate makeup, or shaving, and wearing clean and well fitted clothes.

It can also include taking care of your skin by using an appropriate cleanser and moisturizer for your skin type. You should also protect yourself from the sun with sunscreen and wear sunglasses when outdoors.

The Difference Between Hygiene and Grooming

Hygiene and grooming are both important for teens, but they have definite differences. Hygiene is maintaining cleanliness and health, while grooming is all about taking care of your overall appearance.

Good hygiene habits include cleansing habits that prevent germs and bacteria from entering your body. As we reviewed, good grooming habits include getting a haircut every few months, styling and combing hair neatly, keeping nails neat and clean, wearing appropriate clothing for different occasions, and using the right skincare products.

A good balance between hygiene and grooming is key to developing good self-care habits as a teen. Establish a fun, well-rounded routine that includes daily cleaning habits like showering or brushing your teeth so that you're able to stay healthy as well as look put together on the outside. Maintaining a healthy balance is also essential. There's no need to go overboard with spending too much time or money on specific products or treatments when simple everyday solutions can be just as effective.

Hygiene and Grooming for Girls

For girls like Bernadette, the main grooming steps include washing the face with a gentle cleanser, exfoliation to remove any dead skin cells and dirt if needed and moisturizing the skin to keep it hydrated. Girls can optionally apply makeup.

However, it's worth noting that makeup might be fun to play with but may be harmful in the long run. Some studies show that makeup makes older women look younger because it highlights their youthful features. However, young girls already have these qualities, so makeup actually ages their skin quicker. (Ranscombe, 2018).

Aside from face, young girls may want to groom other areas of the body, such as removing excess hair from legs and armpits. It's recommended to use organic or aluminum free deodorants, as well as washing the hair with a shampoo and conditioner that best suits individual needs. Keeping the vagina area clean is quite important for girls.

The vagina has many parts, such as the labia, clitoris, and vulva, each with a specific function. For example, girls should learn to clean the vulva, which is only the external part of the vagina, with a warm, wet cloth and should only use externally approved soap while avoiding fragranced products.

Also, menstruation can begin anytime between ages 8 and 16, sometimes outside of this range. During this time, young girls should use sanitary pads or tampons to absorb the menstrual blood, but pads are preferred for younger girls. Pads should be changed regularly, and tampons should never be left in for over eight hours. Here are a few more tips:

- Change your underwear daily: Wearing the same pair of underwear for more than one day can cause bacteria to accumulate and lead to infections, so changing your underwear every day is crucial to your health. Choosing cotton-based underwear is also a good idea because it's breathable and helps keep skin dry.

- Wipe front to back: After using the bathroom, wipe from front to back instead of back to front. Wiping from front to back prevents the spread of bacteria from the anus to the vagina, which can lead to infections.

- Don't share personal items: Personal hygiene items such as hairbrushes, towels, razors, and razor blades should not be shared with other people. Sharing these tools can lead to an increased risk of spreading germs or transferring bacteria from one person to another.

- Use Lukewarm water: You don't have to use soaps or other similar products unless it's prescribed by your health advisor, or they are pH-balanced products. Otherwise use lukewarm water to preserve the natural pH balance in this region of the body. Always dry very gently afterwards to keep the area dry, as excess moisture can increase the chance of unwanted bacterial growth, or contribute to skin irritation and itchiness, especially during menstruation.

Overall, as a young woman you will need to understand your body and how to care for it. In puberty, you may experience physical changes, such as acne and body odor, so you need to practice good hygiene habits to help manage these.

Hygiene and Grooming for Boys

For boys like Bradley, some grooming steps may include washing the face with a cleanser too (as this will keep excess oil at bay), using an aftershave balm or moisturizer to soothe any irritation from shaving and replenish moisture in the skin. It can also include styling the hair with a product that provides hold while still looking natural. Boys may choose to groom stray eyebrows or facial hair if desired. Nails should be cleanly trimmed so that bacteria don't build up underneath them.

Boys also need to keep the private areas clean. At birth, a boy's parents have two options: to circumcise their son or not to circumcise. Circumcision is the surgical removal of the foreskin from the penis and can reduce the risk of contracting or passing infections and in order to keep the penis clean and hygienic.

Neither is right nor wrong, but knowing what you have is crucial for hygiene, as an uncircumcised penis requires a different cleaning routine—the skin needs to be pulled back and washed. The testis is also an important area to keep clean. Boys should ensure they hold them away from the water while showering and make sure they dry properly afterward. During puberty, boys may experience erections and wet dreams, which is normal. If a boy notices any unusual symptoms in his genital area, he should visit a doctor to get checked out.

In terms of body hygiene, boys should shower or bathe with warm water at least once a day and use a mild soap or body wash. It's recommended to choose a shampoo and conditioner that is suitable for their hair type, which may or may not be the same as their parents, due to different reasons such as dandruff management. It's important to brush teeth regularly. Finally, boys should know puberty can bring about changes to the body, such as increased body odor, so it's imperative to invest in a good deodorant or antiperspirant.

Overall, teens need to take pride in their appearance! Grooming is something that not only makes teens feel good about themselves but also demonstrates respect for others around them.

Simple Daily Routine Tips for a Busy Schedule

You want to keep your hygiene steps not only effective but also simple enough to easily accomplish in a short amount of time out of your daily routine, without overdoing it. You also want to keep the grooming part in moderation to look good and presentable but still leave enough time for many other activities throughout the day.

Here's a simple routine that can have you up and ready in ten minutes. Before starting, make sure you have all the necessary tools and items nearby, such as a face wash, facial scrub, body wash, toothbrush and toothpaste, deodorant, comb or brush, hair styling products (if applicable), and any other items you'd like to use in your routine.

- Wash your face with warm water and a gentle face cleanser. This will remove dirt and bacteria from your face. Afterward, use a facial scrub to exfoliate dead skin cells if needed, otherwise skip this step. Then rinse off with cool water. Once done with your face-washing routine, apply a moisturizer that is suitable for your skin type to keep it hydrated throughout the day.

- Brush your teeth at least twice a day for two minutes with toothpaste containing fluoride. This will remove food particles from between teeth as well as prevent plaque buildup on teeth surfaces. Don't forget to floss too!

- Apply deodorant under your arms so that you stay smelling fresh throughout the day. Additionally, if desired, you can also apply body lotion afterward if needed to stay moisturized even further during the day. This may be needed especially during dry or hot seasons where environmental factors can be harsh on the skin.

- Style your hair, if applicable, using styling products such as gels or mousses before finishing by combing or brushing through it one last time. This helps keep it looking neat while also providing additional protection against environmental elements such as wind or sun exposure that may damage hair follicles over time if not taken care of properly.

Maintaining good hygiene and grooming routines are essential for a teen's overall physical and mental health and well-being! If these basic steps are performed daily—along with occasional deeper cleaning sessions, you should have no problem staying healthy and looking your best every single day and all year long!

Reflection Questions

What are the key factors of teenage hygiene?

_____

_____

_____

_____

_____

_____

_____

_____

What does your hygiene and grooming routine look like? What might you want to include in a good hygiene routine?

_____

_____

_____

_____

_____

_____

_____

_____

How can you maintain your hygiene in a simple and effective way?

_____

_____

_____

_____

_____

_____

_____

How do you think personal grooming helps you build self-confidence and respect for others?

_____

_____

_____

_____

Chapter 2:

Food, Exercise, and Sleep

Bernadette and Bradley did everything together—they were practically inseparable. But lately, they have been struggling to come up with new ideas to keep them entertained.

One day, Bernadette suggested they take up a new challenge—making healthier lifestyle choices together. They decided to focus on three main areas: food, exercise, and sleep. For food, they agreed to start eating healthier meals and avoiding junk food and sugary snacks. They also agreed to start drinking more water and limit the amount of soda they drank.

For exercise, they planned to go for a 30-minute walk every day. They also took turns picking fun activities like yoga or kickboxing classes together once a week.

For sleep, they decided to each get at least eight hours of sleep each night. They also agreed to limit their time on their phones and computers before bed to help them sleep better.

Bernadette and Bradley were excited to take on this challenge together. They both knew it would take a lot of dedication, but they were confident they could do it. With their newfound commitment to motivate each other on their path to a healthier lifestyle and towards a better version of themselves, Bernadette and Bradley knew their friendship would only get stronger.

What Is Good Food and Eating on Time?

We all know that in order to run a car engine, you'll need to put in good-quality fuel on time. The same exact logic goes for your body. You need to feed your body frequently and accordingly to perform better, stay healthy, and be energized day after day. We will explain different kinds of foods and their nutritional values in this chapter.

Good food is an essential part of a healthy lifestyle. Eating nutritious and balanced meals can provide you the energy you need, help you stay focused, aid your physical and mental health, and keep you strong.

Eating on time is important, too! Your body needs certain nutrients throughout the day to stay balanced and help you perform your best. When you don't eat on time, you may miss out on some of these crucial nutrients, which can lead to fatigue, hunger pangs, or even worse health issues down the line.

Having a regular meal schedule that includes all the necessary food groups ensures your body receives what it needs. Eating breakfast helps you get energized for the day ahead; lunch gives you a boost of energy during the afternoon; dinner fuels you up for whatever comes next; and snacks in between provide extra nutrients if needed.

Not only does eating on time gives you all the nutrition you need, but it can also benefit your overall health. Eating at regular intervals can help regulate metabolism, improve moods, keep a healthy weight, and maintain steady blood sugar levels so that you don't experience sudden drops in energy or cravings for unhealthy foods.

Good food doesn't just taste good—it makes you feel amazing too! Good food is food that provides a balance of energizing nutrients that your body needs to stay healthy. It should consist of a variety of the essentials— fruits, vegetables, whole grains, proteins, and fats. Fruits and vegetables provide vitamins and antioxidants that support overall health, while whole grains contain carbohydrates and fiber. Proteins are the building blocks for bones, muscles, and hormones, while fats provide healthy energy, insulation, and cushioning for cells.

Finally, drink plenty of water throughout the day so your body can stay hydrated.

A well-rounded diet provides all the vitamins and minerals needed to give you the energy to get through your day without feeling sluggish or over-stuffed. Make sure you enjoy your meal as well, as savoring each bite will allow you to really appreciate your food and help your body digest it properly.

Ultimately, it is about nourishing your body with all its needs so that you have enough energy throughout the day while at the same time maintaining optimum health long term. Eating on time prevents nutrient deficiencies and ensures that you have enough fuel for any activities or tasks you need to take care of!

Create Your Own Daily Meal Plan

Eating healthy doesn't have to be a lot of work. The main goal is to be balanced with your meal throughout the day. In turn, you will become healthier throughout the week and into the month. As you become more confident, you will realize it's much simpler and more manageable than you thought.

To help you, you may want to consider spending some time in the kitchen with your parents so you can learn how to use the stove and other appliances safely and properly. They can also teach you how to cook a few simple dishes, and hands-on experience will always allow you to learn more effectively.

Down below are a few meal and snack ideas to get you started as well as a blank weekly table for you to fill in for yourself.

Breakfast	Lunch	Dinner	Snacks
Overnight oats with a sprinkle of cinnamon and fresh fruit	Grilled chicken sandwich with lettuce, tomato, and avocado	Baked salmon with roasted vegetables	Fresh fruit with a sprinkle of lemon juice and a dollop of yogurt
Whole wheat toast with peanut butter and banana slices	Turkey wraps with hummus and veggies	Veggie lasagna with a side salad	Apple slices with peanut butter
Avocado toast with a fried egg and cherry tomatoes	Peanut butter and jelly sandwich with a side of carrots	Teriyaki tofu with steamed brown rice	Hummus and veggie sticks

Breakfast	Lunch	Dinner	Snacks
Blueberry muffins with a side of yogurt	Veggie burger with a side salad	Spaghetti and meatballs with garlic bread	Granola bars
Omelet with spinach and feta cheese	Grilled cheese sandwich with a bowl of soup	Black bean burritos with salsa and guacamole	Trail mix
Protein smoothie with yogurt, banana, and almond butter	Greek-style wrap with feta cheese and olives	Chicken stir-fry with brown rice	Nuts and dried fruit
Pancakes with fresh berries	Quinoa bowl with roasted vegetables	Grilled steak with mashed potatoes and steamed broccoli	Popcorn with a sprinkle of Parmesan cheese

Week 1	Breakfast	Lunch	Dinner	Snack
Day 1				
Day 2				
Day 3				
Day 4				
Day 5				
Day 6				
Day 7				

Week 2	Breakfast	Lunch	Dinner	Snack
Day 1				
Day 2				
Day 3				
Day 4				
Day 5				
Day 6				
Day 7				

Week 3	Breakfast	Lunch	Dinner	Snack
Day 1				
Day 2				
Day 3				
Day 4				
Day 5				
Day 6				
Day 7				

Week 4	Breakfast	Lunch	Dinner	Snack
Day 1				
Day 2				
Day 3				
Day 4				
Day 5				
Day 6				
Day 7				

What Is Considered Exercise?

Exercise is any form of physical activity that increases your body's energy expenditure and muscle contraction. Exercise can range from something as simple as taking a walk or playing a game of tag to something more intense like running or cycling. Regular exercise has many positive impacts on your body.

It can improve physical health and mental well-being and help you feeling your best. Physical health benefits include increased cardiovascular endurance, stronger muscles and bones, improved flexibility and balance, and improved posture. Additionally, exercise can help regulate weight and reduce the risk of obesity and chronic diseases such as diabetes.

Mentally, exercise releases endorphins which create a sense of happiness and relaxation. This can also lead to better sleep quality. Exercise can also be an effective way to reduce stress and anxiety levels. Regular physical activity has been linked to higher concentration levels, sharper memory skills, improved self-confidence, greater creativity, increased resilience in the face of challenges, and a healthier overall outlook on life.

Furthermore, regular exercise can give you a boost in energy and motivation throughout the day by increasing blood flow to the brain (Guo & Zhang, 2022). This may help you stay focused throughout the day rather than feeling lethargic or unmotivated during schoolwork or activities with friends. Exercise is also a fun and different way for teens to socialize with peers while engaging in healthy activities that don't involve sitting in front of screens all day!

Having a suitable and maintainable daily exercise plan is key to getting the most out of physical activity. To start, choose an activity you enjoy—this will make it easier to stick with it in the long run! Next, figure out how often you'd like to work out. For instance, try at least three times per week for 30 minutes each time.

The benefits of a daily exercise plan are numerous: improved overall physical health and mental well-being, increased energy levels, and better sleep quality. You may also experience better concentration, faster recovery from illness, decreased risk of chronic diseases such as heart disease or stroke, weight management, etc. Exercise also helps boost self-confidence because you feel more positive about your body and efforts.

Create Your Own Daily Exercise Plan

You can either work out at home using dumbbells or your body weight or go to a gym. Regardless of how you'll be getting your daily exercise, the key is to make one hour of your daily time that ideally is consistent and maintainable to keep active and healthy. Here are a few exercises you can include in a workout plan:

- Aerobic activity: Cardio exercises are activities that increase the heart rate and breathing rate, such as running, biking, or swimming. These exercises strengthen the cardiovascular system and help burn calories. Do at least 30 minutes of vigorous-intensity aerobic activity three days a week. This could include running, swimming, cycling, jumping rope, or any other sport that gets your heart rate up and makes you feel challenged.

- Bone strengthening: To help maintain healthy bones and combat the effects of osteoporosis later in life, make sure to do some form of weight-bearing exercise 3 days a week. Activities such as jogging, jumping jacks, skipping rope, basketball, tennis, and even walking can help strengthen your bones. And don't forget to work on balancing activities like tai chi or yoga, which can also be beneficial for bone health.

- Muscle strengthening: This type of exercise helps increase bone density and strengthens the muscles, tendons, and ligaments. To build lean muscle mass and add shape to your body, try muscle-strengthening activities such as lifting weights or using resistance bands three days a week. Focus on performing exercises that target all major muscle groups (shoulders, arms, chest, back, legs, and core) for optimum results. When lifting weights, make sure that you start with weights that are comfortable for you and use the proper form to prevent injury while starting with lighter weights. Then gradually increase the amount of weight you're using over time to get stronger and increase muscle mass. Also, consider refraining from consuming any advertised steroid products since they can harm your health. All your body needs are good quality and protein-rich, whole foods.

- Balance and flexibility training: Balance and flexibility training helps to improve coordination, posture, strength, and overall physical health. It also reduces injuries and aid in recovery time after a strenuous exercise session. Balance training focuses on improving your ability to control your body's movements while standing and while in motion This training involves exercises such as single-leg stands, heel-to-toe walks, and side-stepping. Flexibility training enhances your range of motion and the ability to move your joints and muscles through their full range of motion. This can involve static and dynamic stretching, foam rolling, and yoga postures. Including these training sessions into your regular exercise routine can be extremely beneficial for teen athletes. It can help to improve performance and reduce injuries. Balance and flexibility training can also help to reduce stress and improve mental health. It is important to remember that complex balance and flexibility training should be done safely and preferably with the guidance of a qualified fitness professional.

- Overall tips: If desired outcomes include fat loss, then add one to two days of cardio workouts per week; remember to take one day off each week for rest and recovery; drink plenty of water before, during, or after an exercise session and always warm up and cool down properly before and after each workout!

These are a few exercise suggestions. The following pages will help you start your own workout plan. When creating your own plan, choose exercises that target all parts of your body. After a few weeks of following this plan, knowing what to do every day will become second nature. You won't even need to refer to your written plan anymore. Also, ensure that you give yourself enough rest between workouts so that your body has time to recover properly. This will prevent burnout and injury too.

Strength Training Exercises:			
Upper Body	**Lower Body**	**Core and Glutes**	**All Around**
Pushups Triceps Dips Pullups Shoulder press Bent-over rows	Lunges Squats Step-ups Jump squats Reverse lunges	Plank Bridges Side planks Single-leg deadlifts Sit-ups	Burpees Supermans Mountain climbers Plank jacks

Cardio Exercises:		
Low impact	**High impact**	**Extras**
Cycling Elliptical Stair Climbing Hiking Power walking	Jump rope Running Kickboxing Sprints Jump lunges	Swimming Rowing Rollerblading Skiing Dancing

Stretching exercises:		
Upper body	**Lower body**	**All-around**
Neck Rotation	Hip flexor	Child's pose
Shoulder Stretch	Hamstring stretch	Seated forward fold
Chest Opener	Quadricep stretch	Cat/Cow
Standing side stretch	Calf stretch	Downward dog
	Pigeon pose	Spinal twist
	Crossed-leg glute stretch	

Week 1	Exercise Type	Workout Length	Planned Exercises	Completed?
Day 1				
Day 2				
Day 3				
Day 4				
Day 5				
Day 6				
Day 7				

Week 2	Exercise Type	Workout Length	Planned Exercises	Completed?
Day 1				
Day 2				
Day 3				
Day 4				
Day 5				
Day 6				
Day 7				

Week 3	Exercise Type	Workout Length	Planned Exercises	Completed?
Day 1				
Day 2				
Day 3				
Day 4				
Day 5				
Day 6				
Day 7				

Week 4	Exercise Type	Workout Length	Planned Exercises	Completed?
Day 1				
Day 2				
Day 3				
Day 4				
Day 5				
Day 6				
Day 7				

How Important Is Sleep?

Sleep is incredibly important for teens, both mentally and physically. Without enough sleep, it can be hard to focus and concentrate on schoolwork or anything else you do during the day. Not getting enough sleep can also make you moody and irritable, making it hard to get along with friends and family.

On a physical level, sleep helps the body repair itself from the wear and tear of being active throughout the day. It's during sleep that muscles are repaired, hormones are released, and toxins are flushed out of the system. Sleep also helps to boost your immune system, making you less likely to catch colds or other illnesses.

Getting enough good quality sleep is essential for teens who are growing and developing in many ways— mentally, physically, emotionally, and socially. When you get adequate, restful sleep, your body recuperate from daily activities, and your brain process information more efficiently, which helps you perform better academically.

There are four main phases of sleep: light sleep, deep sleep, rapid eye movement (REM) sleep, and dreamless sleep. Light sleep is the phase in which we transition from being awake to sleeping. During this stage, our breathing and heart rate slow down, and our eyes move slowly from side to side. Deep sleep is a deeper stage of restful sleep when our body repairs itself from the day's activities.

During this phase, it is difficult to wake up as brain waves become slower and the body's temperature drops significantly. Rapid eye movement is the most exciting part of our sleeping cycle because, during this phase, we experience dreams. Dreamless sleep is the final stage, where there is no eye or muscle movement, and no dreaming occurs.

To get into a deep state of sleep and improve the overall quality of sleep, consider reducing distractions such as noise, light, and electronic screens. Taking a warm shower before bed helps trigger your body's natural relaxation response, while stretches help increase blood flow which can combat fatigue. Having proper bowel movements before going to bed will also aid in reducing disruptions during your slumber while avoiding going to bed with an empty stomach prevents stomach aches that can cause awakenings throughout the night.

Overall, it's very important to create and practice a lifetime habit consisting of a healthy balance of quality food, a suitable workout plan, and adequate rest to keep you healthy and strong for many years to come.

Reflection Questions

What does your diet consist of?

_____

_____

_____

_____

_____

_____

_____

_____

What times do you normally eat? Do you feel hungry often?

_____

_____

_____

_____

_____

_____

_____

_____

How can you improve your diet?

_____

_____

_____

_____

_____

_____

_____

_____

What are the benefits of eating on time?

_____

_____

_____

_____

_____

_____

_____

_____

Do you try to create a structured meal plan each week?

_____

_____

_____

_____

_____

_____

_____

How many hours of sleep do you get each night?

_____

_____

_____

_____

_____

_____

Do you think getting enough sleep and eating on time can help improve your mental health? Why or why not?

What are some exercises that you might want to try to incorporate into your routine?

_____

_____

_____

How could you improve your eating, exercise, and sleeping routines?

_____

_____

_____

_____

_____

_____

_____

Chapter 3:

Organizing Spaces

Between the two long-time friends, Bradley was a dedicated and hardworking student who always made time for his studies. At the same time, Bernadette was a creative and spontaneous soul who loved to cherish the little joys of life. Despite their differences, nothing could impede their friendship, complementing each other in unique ways.

One sunny weekend afternoon, as the pair sat down to study for their upcoming science test in Bernadette's room, Bradley couldn't help but feel overwhelmed by the clutter surrounding him. Bernadette's floor was covered in clothes, books, and art supplies. Her desk was piled high with papers and half-finished science projects, and her walls were adorned with colorful outer space images and sentimental tokens from her various adventures.

"Bernie," Bradley exclaimed, "how do you manage to study in this chaotic environment?"

Bernadette responded with a shrug and a grin, "It doesn't really bother me, Brad. It's like my own little creative wonderland."

Seeing Bradley's distress, Bernadette started picking up a few things while listening to Bradley. As they sorted through the clutter, Bradley shared some wisdom about decluttering and staying organized, especially for teenagers who often face several challenges, ranging from academic pressure to emotional well-being.

"Being organized can help reduce stress, Bernie. It's been proven that clutter creates a lot of anxiety because our minds perceive it as unfinished business," Bradley explained. "A neat and tidy space makes it easier to remain focused and productive, which is essential for us students."

As they continued to declutter, Bernadette noticed the impact on her mood. The previously chaotic atmosphere was slowly being replaced by a calmer, more serene environment—one that seemed more inviting and conducive to studying.

Bradley further explained, "Staying organized also helps us manage our time more efficiently. As busy teenagers, our lives are filled with schoolwork, extracurricular activities, and social events. Keeping our study materials and schedules organized can help us accomplish tasks faster and ensure we meet deadlines."

Bernadette nodded, realizing the truth in Bradley's words. She had often scrambled to find important papers or forgotten about assignments until the last minute. "Maybe I do need a change, Brad. I'm willing to give organizing a try."

Over the course of the next few weeks, Bernadette and Bradley worked together to develop a simple yet effective organization system for her room and study space. They sorted her papers and belongings—donating or discarding unnecessary items—and created appropriate storage solutions for her clothes, books, and project materials. Furthermore, they devised a calendar and planner to keep track of events and deadlines.

As they completed the transformation, Bernadette noticed an immediate shift in her stress levels, ultimately leading to better study habits, academic performance, and overall well-being. She was grateful for Bradley's guidance and support, realizing that decluttering and organizing not only created a positive change in her room but also in her life.

And so, our tale of two friends concludes with a newfound appreciation for cleanliness and organization. Together, Bradley and Bernadette discovered the true importance of decluttering and staying organized. Their environment played a crucial role in shaping their teenage years and acted as the foundation for personal growth and success.

The Importance of Decluttering and Being Organized

Organizing is like a secret magical spell that helps you transform your messy, chaotic space into a pleasing and efficient haven. Imagine you're in a room full of random objects scattered all around, making it difficult for you to even walk through, let alone find what you're looking for. Now, wave that imaginary magic wand, and voila! Everything is beautifully arranged and instantly accessible. That, dear teens, is the power of organizing!

But let's dig a little deeper.

Organizing involves categorizing and arranging items based on their type, purpose, and how often you use them. For instance, all your clothes can be sorted as casual, formal, or sportswear and then further arranged by color or season. Your books can be grouped by genres or authors in alphabetical order, and school supplies can be allocated to specific containers, so you never have to scramble for a pen or eraser ever again.

Moreover, organizing doesn't just apply to physical objects; it's also vital for managing your time and tasks. Creating a schedule, setting deadlines, and prioritizing tasks can help you make the most of your day and keep procrastination at bay. Here are some fantastic facts and benefits of organizing that will make you want to start right away:

- Saves time: With everything in its right place, you don't have to waste time searching for your keys or that missing sock. Organizing ensures you always know where to find what you need when you need it, giving you more time for fun activities, and friends.

- Boosts productivity: Knowing where your tools and resources are significantly reduces distractions and helps you focus better, which, in turn, increases your efficiency and productivity.

- Enhances creativity: A clutter-free, organized environment allows your mind to think clearly and come up with brilliant ideas. Without the stress of disorganization, your brain is free to wander in the realms of imagination and creation.

- Reduces stress: A messy space can lead to anxiety and stress, as your brain constantly tries to process all the visual clutter around you. Organizing helps you maintain a calm and soothing atmosphere, allowing you to relax and enjoy your surroundings.

- Build healthy habits: Once you start organizing, the habit tends to trickle down to other aspects of your life. You may find yourself making better choices about what you eat or how often you exercise. It can also lead to better time management, all leading to a happier, healthier you.

Organizing is like developing your own personalized system to manage your space, time, and life in a way that suits you best. It may seem overwhelming at first, but once you experience the benefits, you'll be hooked for life. So, gather your friends, put on some upbeat music, and embark on the exciting journey of organizing!

Simple Tips to Start You Getting Organized

Organizing your space is essential for maintaining order in your life. When it comes to organization, you must start somewhere—so why not begin with the following tips?

- Start with a plan: Map out your goals and create an action plan that details the best ways for you to work toward them.

- Designate specific areas for different tasks: Establish separate spaces for studying, working, and relaxing.

- Invest in quality storage solutions: Purchase items that will help you store and organize your belongings, such as shelves, bins, and containers.

- Label everything: Labeling items helps you to easily find the stuff you need while keeping clutter at bay.

- Stick to a schedule: Designate certain days of the week for specific tasks and activities.

- Set aside time to declutter: Take the time to regularly go through your items and discard or donate things that are no longer useful or needed.

- Create reminders: Whether it's a digital calendar, wall planner, or post-it notes—find a way to keep track of what you need to complete.

- Create an inventory: Start by making a list of items that need to be organized, such as papers, books, and clothing. This will help you identify what needs to be done and how long it will take.

- Set realistic goals: Setting realistic, attainable goals gives you a sense of direction and helps you stay on track when it comes to organizing your life and achieving success.

- Create a schedule: A clear-cut schedule can make tracking your daily tasks easier to manage, as well as provide structure.

Important Areas to Organize

Staying organized is an essential skill for everyone, especially teenagers who juggle several responsibilities. Being organized can impact academic success, reduce stress, boost confidence, and create good habits that carry over into adulthood.

Personal Spaces Organization

Having a clean and clutter-free personal space is the first step to an organized lifestyle. A neat bedroom can positively affect your mood and productivity levels. Allocate specific areas in your room for various activities—a study area, a space for relaxation, and a designated place for your belongings.

- Make your bed every day—it can set the tone for an organized day ahead.

- Regularly clean your room, decluttering items and putting things away.

- Organize your desk with essential study materials like books, notebooks, and stationery in easy-to-reach places.

Schedule Organization

Staying on top of your school assignments, projects, and exams is crucial for academic success. Managing your study schedule can help you avoid last-minute studying or cramming sessions and reduce exam stress.

- Use a planner or calendar to record important dates, such as deadlines and exam schedules.

- Break down assignments into smaller tasks and allocate adequate time to complete them.

- Establish a daily study routine and stick to it.

Time Organization

Balancing school, extracurricular activities, hobbies, and social life can be challenging. Effective time management is the key to juggling multiple responsibilities without feeling overwhelmed.

- List down your priorities and allocate time accordingly.

- Avoid procrastination and efficiently use your time, such as completing tasks or studying between classes, or commuting.

- Make use of digital tools, such as apps and websites, to help you manage your time effectively.

Financial Organization

As a teenager, it's essential to learn how to manage your finances. Being financially organized will help you develop responsible spending habits and set a sound foundation for your future financial health.

- Keep track of your income, such as allowances, part-time job earnings, or gift money.

- Create a budget that includes regular expenses, savings, and a small allowance for entertainment purposes.

- Save all receipts and track your expenses to avoid overspending.

Digital Organization

In today's digital age, organizing virtual spaces is just as important as physical spaces. Better digital organization can make your online life more efficient and manageable.

- Regularly organize your computer or smartphone by categorizing files into folders.

- Use cloud storage to back up essential files and documents.

- Unsubscribe from unimportant emails and regularly declutter your inbox.

By following these friendly tips and focusing on these essential areas, teens can develop good organizational habits that will set the stage for a successful and stress-free life, both personally and professionally. Remember: it's never too early or too late to start organizing. So, take the first step, and you'll see the difference it makes in your life, right away.

How to Maintain Your Organized Environment

So maybe now you've finally conquered the mountain of mess in your room (or maybe just a hill), and you're feeling pretty good about it. Now the challenge is to keep it that way. Trust us, keeping your space clean and tidy can be much easier and less time-consuming than having to do a deep cleaning every few weeks.

Create a Daily Tidying Routine

Establishing a simple daily routine can help you maintain order and prevent a mess from building up. Every day, do these quick tasks:

- Make your bed.

- Put dirty clothes in the hamper

- Keep schoolwork, books, and stationery in designated areas (like desks or shelves).

- Clear surfaces like dressers and desks of clutter.

A handy tip is to set an alarm or reminder on your phone to remind you to do these tasks. Doing this should only take a few minutes but can save you hours of cleaning later.

Assign a Place for Everything

One reason clutter accumulates is that we don't have a

designated spot for all our belongings. Assign a specific place for each item in your room and make a habit of returning it to its spot immediately after use. This includes everything from clothing and shoes to electronics and art supplies.

Weekly Mini-Cleanings

Instead of waiting for your space to become a disaster zone, do a quick clean up every week. Spend 10–20 minutes on this and focus on:

- Wiping down surfaces (like your desk, bedside table, and any shelves).

- Vacuuming or sweeping your floor.

- Emptying your trash bin.

These short cleaning sessions will help prevent dirt and dust from accumulating, making your next deep cleaning much easier.

Set Limits for Yourself

Sometimes, our spaces can become cluttered with items we no longer need or use. To avoid this, set some boundaries for yourself:

- Don't accumulate too many clothes or accessories. A good rule of thumb is if you buy something new, consider donating or selling an older item.

- Limit the number of decorative items that can collect dust.

Involve Your Family and Friends

Let your family members and friends know that you're trying to keep your space clean, and ask for their support. They can help remind you to stick to your daily routine and weekly cleanings. Additionally, if you have friends coming over, ask them to respect your efforts by not leaving messes behind.

Reward Yourself

Maintaining a clean space takes time and persistence. But learning to reward yourself for keeping up with your cleaning routine can be motivating. Set rewards like watching your favorite movie, getting a special snack, or spending time doing a hobby you enjoy. This will make keeping your space clean more enjoyable over time.

Now, with these easy tips, you'll sail through the days with a much cleaner and tidier space you can be proud of. So go ahead, high-five your future self for making your life a lot easier.

Reflection Questions

Where do you spend most of your time? Are those areas tidy or messy? Which one is the most cluttered?

_____

_____

_____

_____

_____

_____

What daily and weekly habits can you develop to help keep your space clean?

_____

_____

_____

_____

_____

What good cleaning and organizing habits do you already have or need to improve?

What rewards will you give yourself for keeping up with your cleaning routine?

_____

_____

What can you do to involve your family and friends in
helping you maintain a tidy space?

_____

_____

_____

_____

_____

_____

_____

Chapter 4:

Time Management, Chores,

and Hobbies

Our friend Bradley was a studious and punctual young lad and was like clockwork when it came to managing his time. Bernadette, on the other hand, was the complete opposite. She was notorious for her disastrous time management skills.

One sunny morning, Bernadette came running to the bus stop, huffing, and puffing, her backpack half-open with schoolbooks hanging out. She made it just in the nick of time, with only seconds to spare before the bus zoomed off. Bradley, who had his nose buried in a book waiting for the past 10 minutes, couldn't help but chuckle at his friend's antics.

At school, Bradley noticed Bernadette was always rushing from class to class, barely making it before the bell rang. He realized she was heading toward a disaster that could affect her school life and, potentially, her part-time job at the local movie theater—she'd already been warned once about her tardiness. He decided it was time for his trusty sidekick to learn the life-changing magic of time management.

Bradley, being the supportive friend he was, devised a master plan to tackle Bernadette's terrible time management skills. As they sat eating their lunch in the cafeteria, he explained some simple tips he had up his sleeve.

"Bernie, my dear friend," he began, "I think it's time we address the elephant in the room—your trouble with time management. Have you ever heard of the phrase 'time is money'? Well, for you, it's more like 'time is running out.'"

Bernadette groaned but agreed to listen to Bradley's tips.

"First things first, you need to make a schedule. Plan your day, week, or even month, making sure you allot time for school, chores, work, and, of course, some fun!" Bradley explained, pulling out a colorful planner from his bookbag, much to Bernadette's amusement.

"Next, break down big tasks into smaller ones. By doing this, you can tackle them more easily in the limited time you have. Oh, and don't forget to prioritize! Prioritize,

Bernie! Make a to-do list and focus on completing your most important tasks first before moving on to less urgent ones."

At this point, Bernadette couldn't help but giggle at Bradley's enthusiasm but nodded in agreement.

"And last but not least, Bernie, don't forget to reward yourself! After a week of following your schedule and finishing your tasks, treat yourself to some popcorn and a movie. You can even use your employee discount at the theater!"

Bernadette couldn't hide her excitement at the prospect of having more control over her time, which would make her life a lot less chaotic. She thanked Bradley, gave him a tight hug, and promised to follow his time-management advice from that day forward.

Months passed, and Bernadette began to embrace her newfound time management skills. She was no longer late for school and even earned a promotion at the movie theater for her punctuality and hard work. She had time for her favorite hobbies, and her marks at school improved. Bradley and Bernadette were now a dynamic duo of time management, proving that even the most time-challenged teen can learn the art of punctuality!

As you can see, time management doesn't have to be a chore—it can help make life easier and more enjoyable. With the right attitude and focus, you too, can learn to better manage your time without being stressed.

What Is Time Management?

Time management is organizing and planning how to divide your time between various activities to use your time wisely. It means prioritizing tasks, setting goals, and scheduling your activities so that you can achieve a balance between work, school, hobbies, and other responsibilities. Proper time management prompts you to work in a more efficient and smarter way—not harder—helping you be more productive and efficient.

When you make this a habit and get good at this process, you'll even have some time left to do what you enjoy as well. So, make sure you set aside time for hobbies such as music, dance, sport, games, spending time with loved ones, etc., which all contribute to your well-being as a whole, as well as teach you further social and practical skills.

Now, let's discuss how time management can really help you, especially as a teenager, and break it down into easy-to-understand terms:

- Reduces stress: When you manage your time well, you experience less stress, as you won't be panicking at the last minute trying to finish a task or assignment.

- Boosts self-esteem: Successfully completing tasks can give you a confidence boost. With proper time management, you can efficiently tackle your responsibilities, knowing that you are in control of your life and commitments.

- Improves academic performance: Good time management skills enable you to balance schoolwork with other activities, reducing procrastination and all-nighters, which can lead to better grades and a feeling of accomplishment.

- Encourages healthy habits: When you know how to manage your time better, you're more likely to make time for exercise and other healthy activities, which can have a positive impact on your overall well-being.

- Enhances decision-making skills: Time management involves setting priorities, which means you'll be making decisions based on what is most important to you. This skill is valuable throughout life, as it can help you handle multiple responsibilities and improve critical thinking.

- Fosters balance in life: Managing your time effectively allows you to set aside time for leisure activities, family, friends, and self-care, leading to a greater sense of balance and satisfaction in your life.

- Develops organizational skills: Effective time management requires you to break down tasks into manageable parts, set deadlines, and prioritize steps. These organizational skills can be beneficial in many areas of life, such as college, work, and personal projects.

By practicing effective time management, you can enjoy your busy life, all while juggling school, extracurricular activities, and personal time, without feeling overwhelmed or stressed out. It's all about finding what works best for you, setting realistic goals, and sticking to your schedule.

Remember, good time management skills are key to your success and happiness, both now as a teenager and in the future as an adult. So, start honing these skills today and enjoy the benefits they'll bring throughout your journey!

What to Include for Time Management?

When planning your time management as a teen, considering all the activities and responsibilities you have to account for is vital. Here's a list of common chores, duties, and hobbies that you might need to schedule into your daily or weekly routine. Remember, the key is to balance schoolwork, household chores, and hobbies to have a healthy and enjoyable life.

- Homework and studying: As mentioned earlier, your primary responsibility as a teen is to focus on your education. Allocate enough time each day to complete your homework and study for upcoming tests, quizzes, and exams.

- Household chores: Helping at home not only teaches you valuable life skills but also shows your commitment to being a responsible family member. Some common household chores teens can be responsible for include washing dishes, vacuuming, doing laundry, cleaning their room, and taking out the trash.

- Extracurricular activities: Participation in extracurricular activities such as sports, clubs, or hobbies can help you develop essential social and teamwork skills. Allocate time for practices, meetings, and events to ensure you can fully participate and commit to these activities. Extracurricular activities can also provide a pleasant break from schoolwork and help relieve stress.

- Hobbies: Make time for your personal interests to help you explore your creativity, build new skills, and maintain a well-rounded lifestyle. Hobbies can range from painting, playing a musical instrument, reading, writing, gaming, or anything else that interests you. Be sure to allocate a reasonable amount of time for your hobbies daily or weekly.

- Social life: Spending time with friends and family is a crucial aspect of maintaining a balanced and healthy lifestyle. Make sure you socialize with others, like hanging out with friends, at family gatherings, or attending parties.

- Exercise: Physical activity is not only vital for a healthy body but also for a healthy mind. Incorporate exercise regularly into your life, whether it's going for a jog, playing sports, doing yoga, or working out at the gym.

- Volunteering: Giving back to your community through volunteering can help you develop empathy, appreciation, and valuable skills. Try to allocate some time for volunteering at local organizations, like schools, nursing homes, or animal shelters.

- Part-time jobs: Having work experience while still in school can provide valuable life skills. If you take on a part-time job, consider how it will affect your schedule and ensure you can still manage your other responsibilities effectively.

- Self-care and relaxation: Finally, don't forget to schedule some "me time" to relax and unwind. Include regular breaks that are spent recharging your mind and body to prevent burnout.

In conclusion, time management is key to maintaining a balanced and successful life as a teen. Make sure you allocate time for education, chores, hobbies, and social activities while not forgetting self-care and relaxation. Good luck, and remember, a well-managed schedule can lead to a fulfilling and enjoyable life!

Time Management Tips and Techniques

Time management is crucial for everyone, but it's especially important for teenagers who are juggling school, extracurricular activities, social life, and, eventually, preparing for college and their future careers. Here are some time management tips and techniques for teens, explained in a simple yet engaging manner.

- Create a daily routine: Establishing a daily routine helps you to manage your time effectively. Start by waking up and getting ready for bed at the same time every day. This way, you will get sufficient sleep, and your body will adjust to a regular schedule, making you more focused and alert throughout the day. Divide your day into smaller time blocks, dedicating each block to a specific activity such as school, homework, hobbies, or relaxation.

- Use a calendar: A calendar is essential for keeping track of your commitments, events, and deadlines. Whether it's a physical calendar or a digital one on your smartphone, using a calendar makes it easier to plan your week or month in advance. This helps you to organize your time, avoiding double-booking or missed deadlines.

- Prioritize your tasks: Not all tasks hold the same level of importance, so prioritize them accordingly. Make a list of all the things you need

73

to do and rank them by their importance or urgency. Start with the most urgent or critical tasks and gradually work your way down the list.

- Break down big tasks: Sometimes, big projects or tasks can be overwhelming, making it difficult to start working on them. To avoid procrastination, break gigantic tasks into smaller, manageable chunks. This will make the task feel less daunting, and you'll be able to tackle it one step at a time.

- Set realistic goals: Goals need to be realistic and achievable to avoid disappointment and burnout. Set both short-term and long-term goals, and make sure they are SMART: specific, measurable, achievable, relevant, and time-bound (Yourtherapysource, 2022). This will help you stay focused and motivated. We will review this more in Chapter 16.

- Eliminate distractions: In today's digital age, distractions are everywhere. To manage your time effectively, minimize these distractions first and keep your space clear while you're working or studying. Turn off notifications on your phone, create a quiet workspace, and avoid multitasking.

- Take breaks: It might sound counterintuitive, but regular breaks can boost your productivity.

Studies show that taking abrupt breaks during long tasks helps maintain a constant level of performance (Floras, 2020). So, when you're working on a project or studying for an extended period, take a 5 to 10 minute break every hour to refresh your mind.

- Say no to distractions: As a teenager, it's natural to want to be involved in many activities and events. However, know your limits and practice saying no when you're feeling overwhelmed. If you're already swamped with schoolwork and extracurricular activities, declining a party invitation or a new project can help you maintain better control over your time.

- Evaluate and adjust: Time management is an ongoing process, which means you should always evaluate how well your current strategies are working and make adjustments when necessary. Reflect on your week, identify areas where you could have managed your time better, and make the necessary changes for the following week.

By following these time management tips and techniques, you will be well on your way to becoming more organized and efficient, allowing you to achieve a healthier balance between school, extracurriculars, and other aspects of your life.

Reflection Questions

Do you have good time management skills?

_____

_____

_____

_____

_____

_____

_____

_____

What techniques do you normally use to manage your time? Are they effective?

_____

_____

_____

_____

_____

_____

What areas could you improve in terms of time management?

Do you find it difficult to say no when you're feeling overwhelmed? How could you work on this? How do you keep track of your commitments and deadlines?

_____

_____

_____

Are there any areas where you could be more organized
or efficient? What steps can you take to improve in this
area?

_____

_____

_____

_____

_____

_____

_____

What strategies do you use to prioritize tasks?

_____

_____

_____

_____

Chapter 5:

Communication and

Conversations

Both Bradley and Bernadette were unique in their own way—Bradley was an ambitious young man who dreamed of becoming a professional guitar player, while Bernadette was a confident, free-spirited girl who wanted to be an astronomer.

Even though they were the best of friends, Bradley and Bernadette often struggled in the communication department. They sometimes had trouble understanding each other's perspectives, leading to arguments and misunderstandings. Yet, they couldn't imagine life without the other's friendship, and they knew they needed each other to fulfill their dreams.

One day, while walking home from school together, they came across an old bookstore that they had never noticed before. Intrigued by its mysterious ambiance, they went inside to explore. As they walked through the aisles of ancient books, they stumbled upon a peculiar-looking book half-hidden behind a dusty shelf. It was titled *The Art of Communication: A Guide to Understanding and Connection* by an unknown author.

Their curiosity was piqued, and Bradley and Bernadette bought the book and took it home. They thought that maybe, just maybe, the answers to their communication struggles could be found within its pages. Over the next several weeks, the two friends devoted themselves to studying the book and applying its lessons to their everyday lives.

They soon discovered that the key to effective communication was empathy—the ability to understand and share the feelings of others (Stern & Samson, 2021). By learning to appreciate each other's emotions, they could understand each other's perspectives without judgment, and this made their friendship stronger than ever.

One day, while practicing empathy, Bradley revealed his fear of not being good enough of a performer. He had been struggling with his shyness, which made him question his future to play in front of a crowd. Sensing his discomfort, Bernadette empathetically listened and offered comforting words of encouragement. She shared her own experiences of self-doubt, assuring him that every dreamer faced such challenges.

This sparked a change in their relationship. Bradley and Bernadette had grown more comfortable in sharing their vulnerabilities with each other. Through expressing their deep feelings and insecurities, they became not only friends but soulmates.

In turn, Bradley helped Bernadette with her studies in astronomy. He knew how much she wanted to succeed, and through his artistic insight, he offered unique and creative perspectives on her research. Empowered by their newfound communication skills, Bradley and Bernadette began to thrive in their respective passions.

What Is Communication?

Communication is the process of exchanging information between two or more people through verbal, written, or other signals (Thrive Training and Consulting, 2021). It is an essential part of life as it allows us to express our thoughts and feelings to others and receive their responses in return. Communication helps us maintain healthy relationships with family, friends, and colleagues. It can also help us develop a better understanding of each other's perspectives on various issues.

Communication is especially important for teenagers because it allows them to form meaningful relationships with peers that can last a lifetime. It also helps teens express their needs and wants effectively so they can get what they want out of life. In addition, communication can assist teenagers in making informed decisions as it provides access to different viewpoints, enabling them to weigh all the possible options before coming to a conclusion. By engaging in communication with their peers, teens can form stronger friendships, build empathy toward others, practice active listening skills, and learn how to resolve conflicts peacefully.

Finally, communication is vital for personal growth and development as it enables teenagers to gain greater knowledge and insight into themselves as well as the world around them. Through communication with others, teens can discover different perspectives on certain topics, which may broaden their understanding of certain issues or open their eyes to new ideas they had not previously considered. As such, communication holds immense power for enhancing individual growth among young people by enabling them to engage meaningfully with the world around them.

Effective Communication with Others

Communicating effectively with others is essential for maintaining healthy relationships, solving problems, and expressing yourself clearly. For teens, learning how to communicate effectively can make social situations less stressful and help them forge strong friendships. Here are some tips and guidelines on communicating effectively with others in a friendly and easy-to-understand manner:

- Listen actively: An important aspect of effective communication is active listening. This means not just hearing the words but genuinely trying to understand the other person's perspective. Make eye contact, nod in agreement, and give verbal cues, like "uh-huh" or "I see," to show you are engaged. Avoid interrupting and let the speaker finish their thoughts before responding.

- Pay attention to nonverbal cues: Communication isn't just about words; body language plays a crucial role too. Be aware of your own body language, as well as that of the person you're communicating with. Make sure your facial expressions, posture, and gestures match your message. At the same time, observe the other person's body language to gauge their feelings and emotions.

- Be clear and concise: When expressing your thoughts, try to be as clear and concise as possible. Avoid using jargon or complicated words, and try to be straightforward in your message. This will help prevent misunderstandings and ensure that your point gets across effectively.

- Validate feelings and emotions: During conversations, practice showing empathy and understanding of the other person's feelings. You can do this by validating their emotions, acknowledging their feelings, and showing support. This creates a safe space for honest and open communication.

- Be open-minded: Effective communication requires being open to other people's ideas and opinions, even if you disagree. Show respect and keep an open mind when engaging in discussions. This will help create a positive environment where everyone feels comfortable sharing their thoughts.

- Stay calm and composed: Sometimes, conversations can get heated, and emotions can run high. During these situations, staying calm and composed is necessary. Practice deep breathing, counting to 10, or taking a quick break if you feel yourself getting overwhelmed. This will help you maintain control and communicate more effectively.

- Ask open-ended questions: To encourage conversation and ensure you understand the other person's perspective, ask open-ended questions. These questions require a more in-depth response. This will also demonstrate your interest and encourage further discussion.

- Practice makes perfect: Like any skill, effective communication requires practice. Take every opportunity to engage in conversations and learn from your interactions with others. Reflect on what went well and what could be improved, and apply these lessons to future conversations.

By following these steps, you will be on your way to becoming a more effective communicator with your peers, teachers, and family members. Remember, communication is a two-way street, so always be respectful, patient, and empathetic when engaging with others. As you develop your communication skills, you'll find social situations much more enjoyable and rewarding.

Three Communication Necessities

Communication is a critical skill in life, and as teens, it's vital to learn how to interact with others effectively. Here are three essential communication tactics for teens to master, with explanations and examples to help bring clarity to each concept.

How to Start Conversations

Initiating a conversation can be intimidating, especially for teens who may be shy or unsure about what to say. Here are a few suggestions for getting a conversation started:

- Look for common ground: Start by finding something you have in common with the person, such as a shared interest, class, or activity. This can make it easier to find topics to keep the conversation going. For example, "Hey, I saw you wearing a basketball team jersey earlier; are you a fan too?"

- Start with a compliment: Complimenting someone organically can kick off a conversation by giving the person a sense of appreciation and creating a positive atmosphere. For example, "That's a cool shirt. Where did you get it?"

- Ask open-ended questions: Instead of asking a yes or no question that prompts a short answer, ask a question that encourages the other person to share their thoughts or experiences. Open-ended questions usually start with "how," "why," or "what." For example, "What did you think about the movie we saw in class today?"

How to Ask for Help

It's essential for teens to feel comfortable asking for assistance, whether it's with schoolwork or a personal issue. Here are a few tips on how to ask for help:

- Be direct and specific: Clearly explain what you need help with so the person you're asking understands the issue at hand. For instance, instead of saying, "I don't get this math homework," try, "Can you help me understand how to solve this quadratic equation?"

- Choose the right time and place: While asking for help, consider the setting and make sure the person you're asking is not preoccupied or in a hurry. This will make them more likely to give their full attention to your request.

- Show gratitude: Always express your appreciation for the help you receive, whether with a verbal "thank you" or a small gesture of gratitude. This shows that you value their time and support.

How to Reject Properly

There will undoubtedly be times when teens need to say "no" or turn down an invitation, request, or opportunity. Here's how to do it tactfully:

- Be honest but gentle: When rejecting someone or something, it's crucial to be honest about your reasons while still being considerate of the other person. For example, if you cannot attend an event, say, "Thank you for inviting me, but I have other plans for that day."

- Offer an alternative: If possible, suggest an alternative solution or compromise. This can help soften the blow of rejection and show that you genuinely want to help or participate. For example, if you can't help a friend with their project today, say, "I can't make it today, but I could help you out tomorrow after school."

- Keep it brief and avoid over-explaining: Sometimes, less is more when it comes to rejection. Providing too many details might make it seem like you're making excuses. Stick to a simple "I'm sorry, I can't," followed by a concise reason.

In conclusion, by mastering these three communication tactics—starting conversations, asking for help, and rejecting properly—teens can boost their self-confidence, strengthen their relationships, and navigate various social situations with ease. Practice and persistence are key when mastering these essential interpersonal skills.

Reflection Questions

Do you communicate well?

_____

_____

_____

_____

_____

_____

_____

_____

Have you had to reject someone before, and how did you go about it?

_____

_____

_____

_____

_____

_____

What other communication skills do you think are important for teens to learn?

How can you be more effective when starting conversations?

What tips do you have for asking for help in a respectful way?

How can you be more tactful when rejecting something or someone?

_____

_____

_____

What steps can you take to become a better communicator?

_____

_____

_____

_____

_____

_____

_____

_____

Chapter 6:

General Safety

General Safety is essential for teenagers like Bernadette and Bradley to protect themselves from physical, emotional, financial, or mental harm. Bernadette and Bradley have been friends for a long time, and they both love adventure, trying new things, and pushing each other's limits. One day, Bradley suggested they go cliff jumping at a nearby waterfall.

Bernadette was excited, she had never gone cliff jumping before, and the thought of the adrenaline rush was too much to resist. However, Bradley emphasized that they take precautions and warned Bernadette not to jump before him to ensure the water was deep enough for landing. But Bernadette got overly excited and jumped ahead of Bradley. Unfortunately, she landed badly and injured her leg. Since they didn't have a plan in place in case of emergencies, it took them a while to call for help while Bernadette lay injured.

Bernadette's unfortunate incident is a good example to show the importance of general safety in daily life. Teenagers like Bernadette and Bradley should be careful and take necessary precautions when participating in any activity. They should assess their limits, consider their abilities and avoid taking unnecessary risks.

As you embark on new activities, you should also consider the importance of protecting yourself mentally and emotionally. It's crucial for you to surround yourself with good and trustworthy friends as well as avoid peer pressure-driven situations. You should learn how to say no and always seek help or guidance when necessary.

What Is General Safety?

General safety refers to the practices, rules, and precautions you take to protect yourself and others from accidents, injuries, illnesses, and other potential dangers in your everyday lives. It's all about being aware of your surroundings, making smart choices, and taking necessary actions to minimize risks and harm.

Now, let's dive into some key aspects of general safety and why it's important, especially for teens like you:

- Personal Safety: This involves protecting yourself from physical harm by making informed decisions. For instance, wearing a seatbelt in cars, putting on a helmet while biking, and using the right protective gear when playing sports. Personal safety also extends to mental and emotional well-being, such as standing up against bullying or seeking help from trusted adults when something makes us uneasy.

- Peer-to-peer Safety: As teens, you spend a lot of time with friends at school or in social settings. It's crucial to ensure not only your safety but also the safety of others around you. This means looking out for friends at parties, supporting each other when faced with risky situations, and staying aware of any potential dangers in your environment.

- Digital Safety: Today's world is highly connected, and many activities take place online. Ensuring digital safety means being responsible for our online behavior and protecting personal information. So, be cautious about sharing passwords or personal details, report any suspicious activity, and set privacy settings on social media.

- Home and School Safety: A safe environment, whether at home or school, promotes a positive experience and helps everyone flourish. Familiarize yourself with emergency exits and fire alarms, and learn what to do in case of an emergency. Don't be afraid to report any hazards or suspicious activities to parents, teachers, or authorities.

- Community Safety: As a responsible citizen, it's vital to contribute to your community's well-being. This may involve taking part in neighborhood watch programs, volunteering for local organizations, or teaming up with peers to address and prevent dangerous situations.

So, why is general safety so important for teens? General safety can help you with:

- Prevents accidents and injuries: By following general safety best practices, you can avoid potential risks that could lead to accidents, injuries, or illnesses.

- Promotes independence: Learning to make safer choices can give you the confidence to handle different situations independently, preparing you for greater challenges in the future.

- Fosters responsibility: Being aware of general safety helps you become a more responsible individual by understanding the consequences of your actions and the importance of making informed decisions.

- Builds a positive environment: A safe environment boosts your physical, emotional, and mental well-being, enabling you and your peers to learn, grow, and develop a sense of belonging.

- Ensures long-term well-being: Practicing general safety is an essential life skill that will benefit you beyond your teenage years. It will help you lead a healthy life and teach you to look out for the well-being of others.

How to Practice Proper Safety

Staying safe is essential not only for our physical well-being but also for our emotional and mental health. As a teenager, you can face many challenges and risky situations. That's why it's crucial for you to understand and practice proper safety. Here are some basic steps and helpful tips to ensure you're well-equipped to handle any challenges that come your way!

Be Aware of Your Surroundings

Always be mindful of where you're at and who's around you. Pay attention to what's going on, and trust your instincts. If you feel uncomfortable or sense, something isn't "right," remove yourself from the situation as soon as possible.

Stick With Your Friends

There's safety in numbers. Whenever possible, hang out with friends when going out to social gatherings or exploring new areas. If you're going somewhere alone, let someone know where you're going and when you expect to return.

Avoid High-Risk Activities

Drinking and drug use can lead to dangerous situations and impair your judgment. Choose not to participate in these activities and feel empowered to say "no" when others present or pressure you to join in.

Learn Basic Self-Defense

Being able to protect yourself in a variety of intense situations can be incredibly valuable. Consider taking a self-defense class or learning a few basic techniques online that could help you fend off an attacker.

Maintain Digital Safety

Online safety is just as important as physical safety. Remember to protect your personal information and avoid sharing too much about yourself on social media. Also, be careful about whom you interact with on the Internet and avoid engaging with strangers or giving out your location.

Use Caution Around Strangers

Not everyone has your best interest in mind. Always be cautious when interacting with people you don't know well. It's better to be safe than sorry.

Practice Safe Transportation

If you're driving, always wear your seatbelt, and never text behind the wheel. If you're a passenger, only get in the car with responsible drivers, and avoid riding with people who are under the influence of drugs or alcohol.

Get Help When Needed

If you ever find yourself in a dangerous or uncomfortable situation, don't be afraid to ask for help. Reach out to a trusted adult, which can be a family member, teacher, or counselor. Remember, it's better to ask for assistance than to risk your safety by trying to handle the situation on your own.

Learn How to Read Medication Labels

Many teens take over-the-counter medications without understanding the instructions and possible side effects. Make sure you fully understand what you're taking and any information about dosage or interactions with other medications before ingesting anything. This skill can help you ensure better safety and health practices in the long run!

Remember, safety is about taking necessary precautions and being prepared for different situations. By following these tips and developing a safety-conscious mindset, you'll be better equipped to navigate most future challenges. Stay informed, stay alert, and stay safe!

How to Come Up with a Safety Plan

Creating a safety plan is crucial for you and your family to ensure everyone's safety during emergencies such as fires, earthquakes, and other potential incidents. This section will walk you through some steps to create a safety plan and dive deeper into details and facts that will help you and your loved ones stay safe.

Discuss Safety Measures at Home

Gather your family members and take some time to talk about various emergency situations that could happen at home. Be sure to address the following points:

- Identify escape routes: Look for possible exits and escape routes in each room of your house, and make sure everyone knows where they are located.

- Establish a meeting point: Determine a safe location away from your home where your family should gather.

- Discuss how to use safety equipment: Safety equipment in the home, like fire extinguishers, smoke alarms, and other safety devices, are very helpful, but everyone in the household must know how to use or understand these items.

Be Prepared at Other Locations

Knowing about safety plans at home and places where you frequently spend time is crucial for being prepared. Here are a few areas to consider:

- School: Familiarize yourself with your school's safety plan and evacuation procedures, such as fire drills and lockdowns.

- Part-time job: If you're working a part-time or temporary job, ask your employer about their safety and emergency procedures.

- Grandparents' house: Make sure you're aware of their safety plan and any particular needs they may have.

Know Who to Call for Help

Being able to quickly contact the appropriate person in charge during an emergency is critical. Here are some essential contacts to keep in mind:

- Memorize emergency phone numbers, such as 911 or your local emergency services number.

- Create a list of family and friends you can call for assistance when an emergency arises.

- Know your neighbors, as they can often provide help and support during emergencies.

Practice and Act It Out

Practice makes perfect, and being prepared for various scenarios can be a lifesaver in specific situations. You may encounter these potential incidents:

- Taking care of younger siblings or elderly family members: Ensure you understand their unique needs and have a plan in place to assist them during emergencies.

- Witnessing an incident at a friend's house or in public: Know the appropriate steps to take in case of situations like poisoning, electrocution, or accidents on the street.

Regularly Review and Revisit Your Safety Plan

A safety plan isn't something you create once and then forget. Make a point to regularly revisit the plan with your family to ensure everyone stays informed and prepared:

- Review the plan once a year or more often if needed.

- Update the plan if you move to a new house, change jobs, or if there are other significant changes in your life.

- Test the plan by running drills and discussing hypothetical situations with family members to ensure everyone knows what to do.

By following these steps and regularly reviewing your safety plan, you'll be better prepared to handle emergencies and help ensure the safety of both you and your loved ones.

Reflection Questions

Do you have a safety plan already in place? If so, what does it entail?

_____

_____

_____

_____

_____

_____

_____

_____

What would you want to include or add to your plan?

_____

_____

_____

_____

_____

_____

What are some essential contacts to keep in mind when creating a safety plan?

Are there any potential incidents you could encounter in your daily life that you haven't prepared for?

_____

_____

_____

Review the top three places you visit regularly (home, school, part-time job, etc.) and create a plan for each place.

_____

_____

_____

_____

_____

_____

_____

Chapter 7:

Making Good Friends

A friend is someone who is there for you through the good times and the bad times, supports you, understands you, and genuinely cares about your well-being. Friends are those special people who can share laughter, secrets, and memories with you. A friend is someone you like to spend time with or do activities together because you either enjoy their presence or gain benefit from them. Friends can help you feel accepted and fit in.

It's more fun to go through things having your friends around, and most times, you feel more confident having your friend(s) around. To truly understand the meaning of friendship, let me share with you a little more history between the two longtime teen friends, Bernadette and Bradley.

They first met in kindergarten; Bernadette was trying to solve a puzzle, and Bradley was painting a tour bus on a piece of paper. They caught each other's eye, smiled shyly, and just like that, a beautiful friendship blossomed.

As the years went by, Bernadette and Bradley grew up together. They shared countless experiences. From exploring their neighborhood and building tree forts to joining the school's tennis team and participating in theater plays, these two friends always found joy and comfort in each other's company.

Bernadette was a vibrant, outgoing girl who was never afraid to speak her mind. Her creativity and energetic personality always brought laughter and excitement to their friendship. On the other hand, Bradley was the calm and collected one, always offering a listening ear and sensible advice when Bernadette faced challenges.

Not everything was smooth sailing for Bernadette and Bradley. They had their share of rough times too. In high school, they found themselves surrounded by different groups of friends, and their friendship went through a temporary test. At times, they disagreed about things that seemed important to them as teenagers, like music tastes or fashion choices.

However, amidst these trying times, they learned essential lessons about friendship. They discovered friends do not have to share the same interests or hobbies to support and understand each other. The essence of friendship lies in the ability to accept one's differences and appreciate each person's unique qualities in the relationship.

One memorable experience that stands out in their friendship happened during their junior year. Bernadette was selected to play the leading role in the school's musical production while Bradley was struggling with his math exams. Feeling overwhelmed with her rehearsals and her concern for Bradley, Bernadette almost backed out of the play. However, Bradley insisted she continue with the performance, promising that he would catch up on his math studies and not let fears win his battle with math.

With their unwavering support for each other, Bernadette delivered a stellar performance in the musical, and Bradley aced his math exams. Their success was not just a testament to their individual capabilities but also a shining example of the power of genuine friendship. Like a pillar of strength during challenging times, positive and uplifting friends can prompt you to overcome obstacles and achieve your desires.

As Bernadette and Bradley's story demonstrates, a friend is someone who walks along with you, unconditionally accepts you for who you are, and celebrates your successes while comforting you in your failures. Friends can be a constant source of love, understanding, and belonging throughout your younger years and beyond, making life's journey just that little brighter.

So, the next time you ask, "Who is a friend?" look no further than those special people in your life who make you feel genuinely understood, loved, and supported, like

Bernadette and Bradley, who prove that true friendship is a lifelong treasure.

Friendship Philosophy

Friendship is a beautiful bond that humans share, providing us with companionship, love, support, and so much more. But it also comes with its own philosophy and understanding. Let's dive into the various aspects of friendships and their significance.

First, friendships can come in different shapes, sizes, and relationships. There's the casual friend whom you might hang out with during school or sports but not necessarily share more profound thoughts or secrets. Then, there are close friends with whom you share a deeper connection, spend more time, and confide in about your life experiences. And, of course, your best friend, the person you trust with almost everything and consider as part of your family.

You must understand and appreciate the different levels and qualities of friendship that exist. This way, you can better manage your friendships and not expect too much from someone not on the same level as you. If you try to force a deeper connection with an acquaintance, you might end up feeling disappointed or hurt if the feeling isn't mutual.

Now, let's talk about "Frenemies." You might have heard this term in movies or TV shows—it's basically a combination of these two words "friend" and "enemy."

Frenemies are people who seem friendly but don't have your best interests at heart. They might act nice, but behind your back, they could spread rumors or try to bring you down. Identifying and addressing these relationships is crucial to maintaining a healthy social circle and a positive self-image.

To establish and maintain strong friendships, there are a few key elements you should focus on:

- Communication: Like all relationships, open and honest communication is a must. Share your thoughts and feelings with your friends, and encourage them to do the same.

- Trust: Trust is the foundation of any friendship. Trust your friends with your secrets, feelings, and personal information, and prove yourself trustworthy by keeping their confidence and being there when they need you.

- Respect: Show respect for your friends' boundaries, opinions, and feelings. This means not judging, making fun of, or trivializing their experiences and emotions.

- Loyalty: Stand by your friends and show loyalty in both their presence and absence. Defend them when needed and support them in their successes and failures.

- Empathy: Put yourselves in your friends' shoes and try to understand their feelings, experiences, and perspectives.

- Quality time: Spend time together doing activities that you both enjoy. Build camaraderie through shared experiences, laughs, and memories.

Remember that friendships, like any other relationship, require time, attention, and occasional self-reflection. Reevaluate your friendships, invest in the ones that matter to you, and let go of ones that might be toxic or holding you back.

As you can see, the philosophy of friendship is centered on understanding, mutual respect, and love. As you grow and change throughout your life, so will your friendships. Embrace the journey and enjoy the beautiful connections you make along the way!

Friendship Types

Friends are an important part of our lives; they laugh with us, support us through thick and thin, and sometimes even give us a shoulder to cry on. There are various types of friends, and each plays a different role in our lives. Let's break it down into three main categories: friends for pleasure, utility, and virtue.

Friends for Pleasure

These friends are all about having a good time! They're the ones you call when you want to watch a movie, need a shoulder to cry on, want to play video games, or just hang out at a cafe or the mall. They always help you find a silver lining in a tough situation and make you laugh when you're feeling down. Hanging out with these friends is like a brief escape from your problems, as they can make you forget about the world and enjoy happy moments.

However, friends for pleasure might not always be there for emotional or practical support when you're going through a rough patch. They're great for having fun and creating memories, but deeper connections might be rare in these friendships.

Friends for Utility

These friends come in handy when you need something—whether it's a ride to a party or help with your math homework. They're useful connections who can offer benefits like advice, assistance, or resources. But don't get me wrong—these friendships aren't solely focused on help; they also involve a basic level of trust and loyalty.

Therefore, friends for utility don't always have the strongest emotional connection—they might just share a common goal with you. It's perfectly fine to have these friends, but it's essential to recognize and appreciate friends with a stronger emotional bond, as well.

Friends for Virtue

Now, these friendships are something special. Friends who fall into this category genuinely care about your well-being, and you care about theirs as well. You both inspire each other to be better people and have a deep, emotional connection that goes beyond simple fun or mutual benefit.

These friendships are built on shared values and mutual respect. Your friends, for virtue, will be honest with you, even if it's difficult to hear. They'll encourage you to pursue your dreams and be true to yourself. Having friends like this can help you grow, learn, and determine your likes and dislikes.

In an ideal world, our friendships would be a mix of all three types. We would have friends that make us laugh, provide help when we need it, and encourage us to be the best we can be. However, it is important to remember that friendships often evolve and grow over time, and it's natural for a friend to fit into multiple categories simultaneously.

Recognize and cherish the friends you have in each category, as they all bring something valuable to your life. Whether it's laughter, practical help, or emotional support, friends are the people who shape our lives, and together, we create beautiful memories that last a lifetime.

114

The Science of Making Good Friends

Making good friends is an essential skill for a fulfilling and joyful life. But establishing strong friendships involves more than just meeting new people or hanging out; it requires nurturing connections that comprise shared values, trust, and mutual respect. Let's explore the science behind making good friends and how you can apply it in your daily life.

Choose the Right People

To make good friends, you must first identify individuals who share your interests and values. This can be achieved by joining clubs, going to social events, or participating in extracurricular activities where you can meet people with similar interests. Studies have shown that people who share common hobbies or goals are more likely to have longer-lasting friendships. Associating with those who positively influence you and avoiding those who might lead you down the wrong path is crucial.

Be Approachable and Open-Minded

Your body language and communication skills play a massive role in making new friends. Maintain eye contact, smile, and demonstrate an open body posture to show you are approachable and friendly. Also, be open to different perspectives and ideas, as it will help you connect with diverse groups of people.

Be Supportive and Empathetic

A good friend is someone who understands and cares about the feelings of others. Show empathy by trying to put yourself in their shoes and demonstrating genuine concern for their well-being. Encourage and support their goals and dreams while also offering a shoulder to lean on during tough times. Research has shown that having supportive friends contributes to better mental health and overall well-being.

Be Reliable and Trustworthy

By being honest, transparent, and keeping your promises, you can build trust and credibility in your relationships. A good friend will know your boundaries and respect your privacy. Being consistent and dependable will solidify your friendships in the long run.

Be Willing to Invest Time and Effort

Be open to spending quality time with your friends, either in person or via technology. Additionally, as you get older, staying in touch might become more challenging. However, genuine friendships can endure distance and time as long as both parties will invest in the relationship.

Conflict Resolution

Disagreements and conflicts are inevitable in any friendship. But, the way you handle these situations can either strengthen or weaken your bond. Practice effective communication and assertiveness, and discuss your issues openly and honestly. Remember to be respectful, even in disagreement, as it will help preserve your friendships even in challenging times. We will review more tips in Chapter 8.

Overall, making good friends requires conscious effort and an understanding of what makes relationships thrive. By choosing the right people, being approachable and communicative, actively listening, supporting, being trustworthy and willing to invest time, and resolving conflicts respectfully, you can enjoy meaningful and long-lasting friendships that will enrich your life.

Tips for Finding and Making Friends

Making friends is a vital skill you need to learn as a teen. It can be difficult, but it is achievable if you put in the effort and practice. Here are some tips for finding and making friends.

Start Conversations

A simple yet effective way to make friends is by starting friendly conversations with people. Use the tips we reviewed in Chapter 5 and strike up a conversation with someone new. You can start conversations on general topics such as the weather, a popular movie, or interesting news. Don't be afraid to engage with people at different places, like in school, at hobby sessions, or during group activities. The more people you meet, the higher your chances of finding a genuine friend.

Extend Invitations

When you come across someone you think would make a great friend, don't hesitate to invite them to join you for an activity you both enjoy. This could include watching a movie together, attending a concert, or even offering to help them with their homework. By being proactive, you demonstrate that you are interested in their company, and this can establish the foundation of a strong friendship.

Observe and Understand

As you get to know people, pay attention to their interests and behavior in various situations. This will help you learn more about their personalities, strengths, and weaknesses. Be non-judgmental during this process— your goal here is to find someone who compliments your personality, not to evaluate their worth as a human being.

Join New Activities and Find Common Interests

Try joining a new club or group activity. Not only is this a great way to make friends, but it can also help you learn more about yourself and your interests. Once you have found an activity, take the time to get to know the other members of the group. Ask them questions about what they enjoy most about the activity, and try to find common interests and experiences you can share.

Fun Activities for Teens

Finding, making, and keeping good friends can be a fun and rewarding experience. To do this, engage in activities that promote bonding, improve communication, and encourage positive vibes among peers. Here are some entertaining and enriching activities for teens that can help build strong and lasting friendships:

Sports and Fitness

Participating in team sports or group fitness activities can create a sense of unity and build trust among teammates. Whether it's basketball, soccer, ultimate frisbee, or even yoga and dance classes, these activities teach cooperation, perseverance, and mutual support. Plus, working toward a common goal or improving personal fitness levels together can make for great conversation starters and shared memories.

Hobbies and Interest Groups

From photography and painting to cooking and gardening, there's bound to be a group for any hobby or interest. By joining clubs, workshops, or meetups that align with your passions, you'll be able to connect with like-minded teens and develop friendships organically. Discussing your shared interests can strengthen bonds and ignite a spark for deeper conversations.

Volunteering and Community Service

Helping others is not only fulfilling but can also offer a sense of togetherness and compassion toward your peers. Consider volunteering at a local animal shelter, participating in a beach cleanup event, or serving food at soup kitchens. Through these meaningful experiences, you'll create heartfelt memories with others that can lead to lasting friendships.

Game Nights and Movie Marathons

Gather your friends and bond over some friendly competition with board games and video games. These casual and relaxed environments can encourage interactions while sharing a common goal, which can be foundational to lasting friendships. Alternatively, hosting movie marathons or binge-watching a series together can lead to engaging conversations about the plot, themes, and memorable quotes.

Artifact Hunt and Escape Rooms

Taking part in an engaging and immersive group activity like an artifact hunt or escape room can enhance problem-solving, communication, and collaboration skills. The sense of accomplishment from uncovering an artifact or deciphering a puzzle together can create lasting memories and foster strong friendships.

Talent Show and Karaoke

When teens share their talents, they open up a vulnerability that can create a deep connection between friends. Hosting a talent show or karaoke night encourages self-expression, fosters creativity, and allows everyone to cheer each other on. The memories created during these fun and energetic evenings can spark bonding moments that last for years.

Outdoor Adventures

Explore the great outdoors by going on a hike, bike ride, or camping trip. These activities provide opportunities for shared exploration, overcoming obstacles, and enjoying breathtaking scenery together. Bonding over these thrilling experiences can form memories that strengthen the foundation of wonderful friendships.

Overall, by participating in these fun activities, teens can build a solid friendship circle that will support them through various life stages. And remember, always be yourself when forming friendships, as loyal friends will love and appreciate the real you.

Reflection Questions

Do you consider yourself to be a good friend?

Do you think it's more important to have quality friends or a higher quantity of friends? Which do you currently fall under?

_____

_____

_____

What skills could you improve to be a better friend?

_____

_____

_____

_____

_____

_____

What are the traits you look for in a good friend?

_____

_____

_____

_____

_____

What positive traits can you offer? Which traits would you like to improve?

Chapter 8:

Disagreements and

Arguments

One sunny afternoon at the park, Bernadette and Bradley were hanging out when a disagreement arose. Bernadette avidly believed that their town's local library should be open later. Bradley, on the other hand, argued that it would be a waste of resources because most people wouldn't want to visit a library late at night.

As the argument began to heat up, both friends felt that they had to defend their points of view, and it seemed like this disagreement could harm their friendship. However, they both remembered the valuable lessons they had learned from their parents and teachers about effective communication and conflict resolution. So, Bernadette and Bradley decided to take a step back and practice some skills they had learned in order to handle the argument in a peaceful and effective manner.

The first thing they did was to take a deep breath, make eye contact, and calmly express their feelings. They both used "I" statements, preventing them from sounding accusatory or blaming.

Bernadette said, "I feel that the local library should be open later in the evenings because it would give people more opportunities to use the resources and services."

Bradley shared his point of view, "I see your point, but I believe that most people might not want or need to be at a library late at night and that it could be a waste of resources."

Then they start to listen actively to each other without interrupting. They knew it was essential to understand the other person's perspective fully. So, they asked questions for clarification and repeated what they heard to ensure that they had understood correctly.

After listening to each other, they realized they had some common ground—they both wanted what was best for their community. So, they brainstormed possible solutions that could satisfy both of their concerns.

Together, they came up with the idea of a survey that would gauge the interest of the town's residents in having the library open later. This way, they could determine if this move would indeed be helpful or a waste of resources. They shared the idea with the librarian, who was impressed with their critical thinking skills and decided to implement the survey.

The key to effectively handling their argument was open communication, active listening, and seeking common ground. Instead of focusing on their differences, Bernadette and Bradley saw their intentions were the same—to create a better community.

At the end of the day, Bernadette and Bradley not only resolved their disagreement but also deepened their friendship. Through their journey, they discovered disagreements are completely normal, but the way they are handled can affect the quality of their relationships. So, next time you find yourself in a disagreement with a friend, take a moment to practice effective communication and conflict resolution skills, and you might just strengthen your bond with that person.

Disagreements vs. Arguments: What is the Difference?

You must have noticed how people sometimes get into heated exchanges, right? It's pretty normal, but do you know the difference between a disagreement and an argument? If not, no worries. Let's explore these two concepts.

Disagreements Explained

A disagreement is when two or more people have different opinions, viewpoints, or beliefs about a particular topic, issue, or situation. It happens all the time in our daily lives because everyone is unique; therefore, we all perceive things differently. Here are some key points to remember about disagreements:

They are a natural part of human interactions: You can't expect everyone to agree with you all the time, right? We all have different backgrounds, experiences, values, and perspectives that shape our thoughts.

They can be healthy: As surprising as it may sound, disagreements can be good! They allow us to share our ideas, learn from others, and expand our horizons. And who knows, you might change your mind or reinforce your belief after considering someone else's viewpoint.

They don't have to be confrontational: Disagreements can be resolved calmly and respectfully without turning into full-blown arguments. The point is to maintain an open mind and be respectful when expressing your opinion.

Arguments Explained

An argument, on the other hand, is a heated exchange where two or more people are trying to prove that their perspective is right or better than the other. They often involve powerful emotions, raised voices, harsh words, and sometimes even aggressiveness. Here's what you need to know about arguments:

They can often be destructive: Unlike disagreements, arguments can lead to hurt feelings, animosity, and even a rift between people. It's because arguments are more focused on winning the debate rather than understanding the other person's perspective or reaching a compromise.

They might not be logical: While arguments can start as simple disagreements, they often escalate to the point where people attack each other's character, bringing up past issues or using faulty reasoning to prove their point.

Sometimes, they are necessary: Yes, you read it right. Sometimes we need to stand up for what we believe in, especially when encountering harmful ideas, unfairness, or injustice. However, it's crucial to remember that we should always try to communicate with respect and be open to listening.

So, what's the takeaway?

The crucial difference between disagreements and arguments is the way we approach the conversation and how we choose to express our opinion. Disagreements are more about understanding, learning, and respecting others, while arguments are emotionally charged exchanges aimed at winning and proving a point.

Now that you understand the distinction between disagreements and arguments, why not practice more open-mindedness and active listening in your discussions with others? It's an excellent way to foster healthy conversations, build stronger relationships, and develop essential life skills! Good luck, and always remember to stay respectful and cool-headed, even in the heat of the moment.

How to Diffuse Confrontations

Handling arguments or disagreements is a valuable life skill that everyone should learn, especially during teenage years, as it helps build strong relationships and promotes personal growth. As you can see from Bernadette and Bradley's example, arguments can get out of hand quickly. When faced with such a situation, a healthy conversation is vital to learning how to handle the argument effectively and avoid escalating the conflict.

Here, we will explore some effective ways to handle arguments and resolve disagreements, according to Thrive Training and Consulting (2021).

- Stay calm and composed: It's natural to feel heated and defensive during an argument, but staying calm can prevent the situation from escalating. Take deep breaths, count to ten, and remind yourself that resolving the issue is more important than winning the argument.

- Be respectful: Show respect for the other person's feelings and opinions, even if you disagree. Avoid name-calling, shouting, or making fun of them. Remember, the goal is to find a solution, not to make the other person feel bad.

- Listen carefully: Pay attention to what the other person is saying and acknowledge their points. Avoid interrupting or jumping to conclusions, as this can create misunderstandings and increase tension. Instead, listen with empathy and put yourself in their situation.

- Use "I" statements: Express your own feelings and opinions using "I" statements to minimize blaming and accusing. For instance, let's say your mom came home late from work. Instead of saying, "Mom, you're always late!" try saying, "I feel that I don't get to spend enough time with you when you're late from work most days. Is there anything I can do to help to see you more at home? (etc.)"

- Find common ground: Identify the common interests or goals between you and the other person. This will help create a sense of teamwork and cooperation, making it easier to find a compromise.

- Be open to compromise: In most disagreements, both parties can benefit from compromising. Be flexible in your thinking and be open to finding a solution that works for both of you.

- Try to imagine what it's like for them: If you want to effectively handle an argument, it is important to put yourself in the other person's shoes. Imagine their viewpoint—their feelings, opinions, and point of view. This will help you better understand their perspective and why they feel the way they do. It also allows us to be more compassionate, as it reminds us that everyone deserves respect.

- Ask the other person questions about the reasons they have come to a certain decision: Asking questions can prompt you to learn more about the other person's point of view. It also gives them a chance to explain why they feel a certain way, which can help you understand their position. Just be sure to phrase your questions in a respectful manner and avoid making assumptions or jumping to conclusions.

- Be creative when thinking up solutions: Be creative in your problem-solving efforts—there is usually more than one solution to any problem.

Be daring and come up with innovative ideas that both parties can agree on.

- Don't forget to breathe and invite your friend to breathe too: In a heightened situation, it's easy to forget about basic needs such as breathing. Take a few seconds before speaking to take some deep breaths and invite the other person to do the same. This can help clear your mind and bring a sense of calmness to the situation.

- Model neutral language: Using neutral language when discussing matters can help keep things civil and allow both parties to feel respected. Avoid using language that puts anyone down or comes across as overly aggressive. Instead, focus on finding a productive solution to the problem at hand.

- Separate the person from the problem: Remember that the problem is separate from the person. Blaming, attacking, or insulting one another won't help resolve anything. Instead, focus on discussing the issue at hand and work together to find a solution.

- Be a calming agent: A great way to handle an argument is to be a calming agent. Speak and act in a way that is respectful, professional, and empathetic. This will show that you care and will cooperate in order to find a resolution.

- Take a break if needed: Sometimes, taking a brief break can help both parties calm down and approach the situation with a fresh perspective. Remember, it's more important to resolve the issue than to resolve it right away.

- Agree to disagree: In some cases, finding common ground or reaching a compromise is impossible. In these situations, it's okay to agree to disagree and maintain a respectful relationship.

- Apologize when necessary: If you've made a mistake or hurt the other person's feelings, be willing to apologize and take responsibility for your actions. This demonstrates your maturity and understanding of the situation.

- Reflect on the situation: After an argument, take time to reflect on the interaction, what you learned, and how you can improve your communication skills in the future.

By practicing these techniques, you can effectively handle complicated conversations in a friendly and peaceful manner. Remember, every disagreement is an opportunity to learn, grow, and strengthen your relationships with others.

Dealing With Family Tensions

Dealing with family tensions can be tough, especially for teens. Whether your family is traditional nuclear, separated, extended, or blended, you will experience certain situations that will require further skills to tackle, so you can rise above your differences or difficult situations and still be happy. Here are some effective ways to help you handle family tensions in a friendly and easy way to understand.

- Communication is key: If something is bothering you, speak to someone and talk out loud about it. Don't ever feel that your age is a limitation to convey your concerns, as the youngest member of the family can also add valuable points at times, that grownups may miss to realize. Speak up and express your thoughts and feelings in a calm, respectful manner. Don't take sides and reference the communication techniques that we've explained earlier in this chapter, and in Chapter 5.

- Be a good listener: Just as it's essential for you to express your thoughts, it's equally important to listen to others. Practice active listening skills by showing that you're paying attention by making eye contact, nodding, and not interrupting. Try repeating what you've heard to make sure you've understood correctly. This will make your family members feel heard and acknowledged, leading to a more productive conversation (Shenfield, 2017).

- Spend quality time together: Family bonding is crucial for easing tensions. Especially for a separated family, it's important to spend equal amount of quality time with both parents. Allocate time for family activities that you all enjoy, like movie nights, playing board games, or cooking dinner together. These experiences can nurture positive feelings and connections among family members.

- Seek outside help: If you feel like family tensions are overbearing and can't be resolved on your own, it's okay to ask for help. Seek guidance from a trusted adult or a professional, like a teacher, counselor, or therapist. They can provide you with valuable insights and support on how to handle family tensions effectively.

- Tackle the larger issue: Sometimes, recurring family tensions may stem from unresolved larger problems. Try to identify the root cause of the tension and work together as a family to solve these issues. This will not only improve the current situation but also prevent similar tensions in the future.

By incorporating these strategies into your life, you can

effectively handle family tensions and create a more harmonious environment for those in your life. Remember that conflict is a natural part of life, and it's not about avoiding it but managing it constructively.

Reflection Questions

Do you think you get into arguments often? What do you think may cause this?

_____

_____

_____

_____

_____

_____

_____

Which skills do you think you need to work on?

_____

_____

_____

_____

_____

Which skills do you think you already do well?

How do you communicate with your parents? How would you describe your relationship with them?

How do you think you can use these communication techniques to resolve family tensions in a more effective way?

Chapter 9:

Mood Swings and Emotions

One rainy afternoon, Bernadette noticed that her best friend, Bradley, seemed to behave unusually. Bradley was always a bit shy but normally a very positive and happy guy. He had become more irritable and sadder all of a sudden. Just a moment ago, they were laughing and joking about a funny video that went viral, and in a trice, Bradley's mood shifted into quiet reflection and a hint of frustration. These sudden changes in his emotions had become more frequent over the past few weeks.

As the weeks went by, Bernadette noticed that Bradley's mood swings were affecting not only their friendship but also his daily life. He wasn't performing as well in school as usual, and over time, Bernadette saw him begin to isolate himself from their group of friends. Fearful of losing their close bond, she mustered up the courage to ask Bradley what was going on.

Bernadette explained to Bradley that she had noticed his mood swings and was concerned about their impact on his life. Using empathy and understanding, she asked if he was open to discussing his feelings and if there was anything she could do to help.

Hesitant but touched by her concern, Bradley admitted he had been struggling with stress from school, his part-time job, and some family issues. He realized that his sudden mood swings were likely a coping mechanism for the immense pressure he was feeling.

To help him deal with these fluctuations in his emotions, Bernadette suggested some research and strategies to cope with his stress more effectively. They agreed that talking about their problems, staying active, and incorporating stress-relief techniques like mindfulness and deep breathing exercises could positively impact their stress levels and mood swings. They even promised to keep each other accountable and remind one another about self-care. Bradley admitted, he wished he had reached out for help sooner!

Over time, with the support of Bernadette, Bradley's mood swings became less frequent, and together, they built a stronger connection as friends.

Mood swings and emotions can be difficult to handle at times, but with the right approach, it is possible to understand and manage them in a healthy way. By understanding the different factors that can cause mood swings, like stress and hormones, teens like Bernadette and Bradley can support each other and learn to cope with these common emotional fluctuations in healthy and constructive ways. As a result, they can develop stronger emotional intelligence and resilience that will help them throughout their lives.

What Are Mood Swings?

Now, let's dive into what mood swings are, why they happen, and how to deal with them.

Mood swings are pretty much what they sound like— when our emotions change quickly or suddenly without a specific reason (Spencer, 2018). One moment, you're feeling super happy or chill, and the next, you might be feeling sad, angry, or even ecstatic. These rapid shifts in emotions can be confusing, frustrating, or even scary. But don't worry, it's pretty normal, especially when you're a teenager.

Why do mood swings happen, you ask? Well, there are a few reasons:

- Hormones: As a teen, your body's hormones are all over the place. These hormones, like estrogen and testosterone, play a significant role in regulating our emotions (Monroe, 2012). So, when they're constantly changing, our emotions can change too. Remember that everyone goes through this stage, and it's all a part of growing up.

- Brain development: Did you know that your brain is still developing throughout your teenage years? That's right—your brain doesn't fully mature until your mid-20s. This means that the parts of your brain responsible for controlling emotions and decision-making are still growing, which can sometimes make emotions seem more intense and harder to control (Raising Children Network, 2017).

- Stress: Life can be stressful at times, especially as a teenager. School, friendships, relationships, and just figuring out who you are can all contribute to mood swings. When we're stressed, our emotions can become more exaggerated, leading to stronger mood swings (Morin, 2015).

- Lack of sleep: Getting enough sleep is super important for your brain to function properly, and not getting enough can lead to mood swings. Teens need around 8–10 hours of sleep each night, and if you're not getting that, it may be harder for you to regulate your emotions (Morin, 2015).

Now that you understand what causes mood swings, let's explore some ways to cope with them:

- Practice self-awareness: Pay attention to your emotions and feelings and acknowledge them. Recognize that mood swings are normal and that it's okay to feel many emotions—just remember not to take them out on others (Morin, n.d.).

- Self-care: Take care of yourself physically, mentally, and emotionally. Eat well, get plenty of sleep, exercise, and do things you enjoy.

- Talk about it: Chat with your friends or family members about your mood swings. Sharing your feelings and getting some support can be really helpful.

- Relaxation techniques: Learn techniques to help you relax when you're feeling overwhelmed, like deep breathing exercises, meditation, or even just listening to music (D'Amico, 2021).

- Get professional help if needed: If your mood swings are overwhelming, affecting your daily life, or you're feeling down for an extended period, it might be useful to talk to a mental health professional for support.

Overall, mood swings are normal, especially during this time in your life. They're the result of hormone fluctuations, brain development, stress, and sometimes even lack of sleep. Remember to practice self-awareness, take care of yourself, and seek help if needed. You're not alone in this journey, and you can absolutely learn to navigate these emotional roller coasters.

Reflection Questions

Do you experience mood swings? If so, how often?

Do you think your emotions are affected by hormones, brain development, stress, and/or lack of sleep?

Can you tell when your mood is affected by outside factors?

What strategies do you use to cope with mood swings? Do they work for you?

What strategies do you think you can include to better manage your mood swings?

What strategies do you think you can include to deal or help someone else's mood swings?

Chapter 10:

Making Decisions

One summer afternoon, as they were hanging out by the lake, Bradley brought up an exciting opportunity to volunteer at a local charity event happening the following weekend. The due date for registration was the next day, and the event promised an enriching experience, free food, and even a chance to meet some famous motivational speakers. Bernadette was just as interested but hesitated a bit as she pondered whether she should commit.

Bradley, being the decisive person he was, went home, checked his schedule, and immediately signed up.

Bernadette, on the other hand, decided to wait and think it through before making up her mind.

As the days went by, Bernadette was still unsure if she should join the event. With the deadline long past, she kept pushing the decision off, thinking that she still had time to join at the last minute. In contrast, Bradley couldn't wait to participate and frequently shared updates about the event with Bernadette, trying to convince her to sign up too.

Finally, the day of the event came. Bradley eagerly got dressed and headed out early, while Bernadette stayed at home, her indecisiveness getting the best of her. At the charity event, Bradley not only had a blast participating in the activities, bonding with new people, and enjoying scrumptious food, but he also met one of the motivational speakers who became his mentor.

As Bradley shared his unforgettable experience with Bernadette, she couldn't help but feel a pang of regret for not deciding on time. She realized that by not being decisive, she had missed out on an incredible opportunity that could have created unforgettable memories and opened new doors for her.

This story highlights the importance of making timely decisions. Often, life offers us exciting opportunities that come with a deadline. By taking your time to think it over, it's easy to miss out on these chances. When you keep delaying decisions or waiting for something better to come along, you end up with nothing at all.

Teenagers like Bernadette should understand that being decisive can lead to personal growth, new experiences, and lifelong memories. Life is too short to let opportunities slip by, and by making on time decisions, you take control of your own journey, molding the person you become.

In conclusion, Bradley and Bernadette's story serves as an eye-opener for teenagers to realize the importance of decision-making. Time waits for no one, and indecisiveness can cost you dearly. Don't let the fear of making the wrong choice hold you back. Instead, embrace the possibilities, make thought-out decisions, and learn from the experiences you gain, for that is the essence of life.

The Process of Making Decisions

Making decisions is like sorting through different options and picking one that best suits our needs, goals, or values. Each person has a unique decision-making style, but some standard steps can help us make better choices in a more organized manner. Let's dig into the details:

- Identify the decision: Clarify what precisely the decision is about. The best way to do this is by asking yourself, "What am I trying to accomplish?" or "What problem am I trying to solve?" By clearly defining the decision, you'll better understand the context and what's at stake.

- Gather information: The more data and knowledge you have about the situation or option, the more likely you'll choose something that works. It's like going grocery shopping with a list vs. wandering the aisles aimlessly. Collect all the essential details required to make an informed decision, so you're well-prepared.

- Analyze options: With the proper information, you can now explore different alternatives (known as your "options set.") Think about the potential choices, their pros and cons, and how well they align with your goals or values. It's like trying on different pairs of shoes to see which ones fit and look the best.

- Decide: Once you've evaluated different options, it's time to pick one. This step might feel intimidating, but remember that no decision is perfect, and it's okay to change your mind later if necessary. Trust your gut and the facts you've gathered throughout the process to make a confident choice.

- Take action: Now that you've committed to a decision, it's time to put it into action. Brainstorm the steps and resources needed and create a plan to execute your decision. Let the world see the fantastic choice you've made.

- Review and learn: Finally, reflect on the outcome of your decision. Did it have the desired effect or solve the problem? Were there any unexpected consequences? Learn from your decision-making experiences to improve your skills for future scenarios.

Remember, making decisions is an ongoing process, and there's always room for growth. Be mindful of your choices, learn from your experiences, and keep practicing: you'll get better at deciding as you go.

Your Own and on Time Decisions

You might wonder, why should I bother? Can't someone else make decisions for me? Well, as you grow older, making decisions will become an inevitable aspect of your life. Let's dive into the reasons making timely and independent decisions is so important.

- Builds confidence: When you take charge and decide on your own, you develop self-confidence. This feeling of accomplishment will help you believe in yourself and trust your abilities. Plus, you'll be prepared to tackle challenges that come your way in the future.

- Develops problem-solving skills: Decision-making goes hand in hand with problem-solving. You build your critical thinking abilities when you analyze different options and their potential outcomes. These skills are super useful in school, careers, and everyday life.

- Establishes independence: Feeling dependent on others can be frustrating. By deciding for yourself, you learn to rely on your own judgment, which helps you become more independent and self-reliant. Independence is a key element in the journey of personal growth and self-discovery.

- Enhances responsibility: Making your own decisions means taking responsibility for their consequences, whether good or bad. This is a vital life lesson for becoming a responsible adult. Remember, with great power (of decision-making) comes great responsibility.

- Improves time management: Procrastinating and delaying decisions can lead to missed opportunities, added stress, and poor outcomes. Making timely decisions helps you to manage time better and avoid a last-minute rush that may cause hasty choices.

- Promotes personal growth: Every decision, big or small, shapes your life experiences. Making decisions allows you to learn from them, whether it's from a mistake or a triumphant choice. It's a cool way to grow, develop, and form your unique personality.

- Enhances adaptability: The world is always evolving, and making quick and effective decisions helps you stay adaptable to change. As the saying goes, "Change is the only constant." So, developing the ability to make decisions, can make you more flexible and prepared for uncertainties that life may throw at you.

- Empowers you: Last but not least, being in charge of your decision-making skills gives you control over your life. It's about taking charge of your destiny and steering your life in the direction you want. Isn't that empowering?

Mastering the art of decision-making is a critical life skill that helps build confidence, develop problem-solving capabilities, establish independence, and much more. So go ahead, flex those decision-making muscles, and create a bright and promising future for yourself.

A Growth Mindset Dealing with Your Wrong Decisions

We all make wrong decisions sometimes, and that's totally okay. It's just part of being human. The important thing is how we deal with those decisions and learn from them. Having a growth mindset can make a world of difference in these situations. Curious about what that means and how it can help you?

A growth mindset is a belief that with hard work, effort, and dedication, you can learn new skills and improve upon your abilities. It's about being open to accepting mistakes and failures as part of the learning process (Schwarz, 2017).

To adopt a growth mindset, it's important to remember that making wrong decisions doesn't mean you are a failure; it simply means you made the wrong choice and need to adjust accordingly. It can be difficult to accept our mistakes, but by doing so, we can move on and become better for it.

When dealing with wrong decisions, it's also important to take the time to reflect and find out what went wrong. This can help you better understand your mistakes and learn from them so that you don't make the same ones again. Here are a few more ways you can cultivate a growth mindset:

- Accept your mistake: The first step in dealing with a wrong decision is acknowledging the fact that you made a mistake. Take responsibility for your actions, and do not dwell too much on what could have or should have been.

- Analyze the situation: Try to understand why you made the wrong decision. What factors led to it, and what could you have done differently? This analysis will help you gain insights into your decision-making process, which you can then use to improve in the future.

- Learn from your mistake: Making a wrong decision can be a terrific learning opportunity if you're willing to embrace it. Every mistake can teach you something valuable that will help you grow and become a better decision-maker.

- Make a plan to move forward: Revisit your original goal or objective and come up with a new plan to achieve it. Figure out what steps you can take to avoid making the same mistake again and how you can improve your overall decision-making process.

- Forgive yourself: We all make mistakes, but dwelling on them won't do any good. Instead, forgive yourself, learn what you can from the experience, and make a commitment to do better next time.

Overall, this mindset means believing that you can improve yourself, your skills, and your abilities through hard work, effort, and dedication. This mindset is incredibly important for dealing with wrong decisions since it can help you:

- Stay positive: A growth mindset encourages you to view mistakes as opportunities to learn and grow rather than as personal failures that define who you are.

- Embrace challenges: People with growth mindsets see challenges as chances to expand their abilities, which means they're more likely to improve from difficult situations.

- Stay motivated: When you have a growth mindset, you're more likely to bounce back quickly from setbacks and maintain your motivation to achieve your goals.

- Improve problem-solving skills: A growth mindset can help you approach problems with curiosity and determination, leading to better problem-solving strategies and more effective decision-making.

- Boost self-esteem: With a growth mindset, you believe you can improve and become better at anything you put your mind to, which can lead to higher self-esteem and greater overall happiness.

So, next time you find yourself making a wrong decision, try to apply these tips and embrace your growth mindset. Remember, it's not the mistakes that define us; it's how we learn and grow from them that truly makes a difference. Don't be afraid to make mistakes, and never stop learning.

Reflection Questions

In what areas do you struggle to make good decisions?

_____

_____

_____

_____

_____

_____

_____

_____

What can you do to improve your decision-making process?

_____

_____

_____

_____

_____

_____

Do you have a growth mindset?

In the future, how can you look at mistakes as learning opportunities?

_____

_____

Take a mistake from the past and consider how it has helped you grow. What did you learn?

_____

_____

_____

_____

_____

_____

_____

_____

Hope you're enjoying this book so far 😊

As an author who thrives to provide value to my readers, it's important to me to know your opinion.

Also, this is your chance to help others find this information. By leaving a review, you will be part of something much bigger, and will be helping many other parents and young people.

Thank you for joining me to build a stronger community, and skilled future generation, who will continue to make a better world!

Please go ahead and leave your review by clicking on your region-specific link below:

https://www.amazon.com/review

https://www.amazon.ca/review

https://www.amazon.co.uk/review

Now let's get back to our book …

Chapter 11:

Building Confidence

Bernadette and Bradley were enjoying their high school years, exploring their interests, discovering their passions, and supporting each other every step of the way. Despite being different in many ways, they were united by a single, powerful trait—self-confidence.

Bernadette was a science savvy gal who loved to talk about astronomy related topics for hours; everyone around her admired her science project presentations. Bradley, on the other hand, was a talented musician known for his enchanting tunes played gracefully on the guitar. Although their talents differed, their self-confidence brought them together in pursuing their passions.

One day, their high school announced an upcoming talent show. Bernadette and Bradley were eager to participate and showcase their abilities. As the big day approached, they realized that self-confidence was the key to conquering their nerves and putting on their best performances.

That particular afternoon, Bernadette, who normally enjoyed being in front of an audience, could unusually feel the butterflies in her stomach when she took to the stage. Even though her hands were shaking, she told herself that she had faith in her scientific knowledge transfer and demonstration skills and had meticulously prepared her presentation. Through these positive thoughts, suddenly, her usual self-confidence began to shine through her azure eyes, and as she began her speech about outer space, the audience was enthralled by the amount of knowledge and passion she presented. The applause she received at the end of her presentation reaffirmed her belief in herself and brought a smile to her face.

Bradley, being shy by nature, expected to feel the stage fright as he always did in the past and similar situations. So, he had done some self-talk, breathing techniques, and preparation beforehand. And as predicted, he felt a mix of excitement, anticipation, and nervousness as he walked up on stage with his guitar. However, he decided taking a deep breath, clearing his thoughts, and reminding himself of the countless hours he had spent practicing and perfecting his melodies. With newfound confidence, he began strumming his guitar and delivered a heartwarming performance, leaving the audience mesmerized.

Later, as they rejoined each other backstage, Bernadette and Bradley discussed the importance of self-confidence. They both understood that in addition to their innate talent, their faith in themselves had played a significant role in overcoming their stage fright and giving remarkable performances.

Self-confidence is crucial for every teenager as it is a steppingstone to success in various aspects of life. Whether it be academics, sports, or other extracurricular activities, a powerful belief in oneself helps conquer fears, battle insecurities, and overcome obstacles. When people have confidence in their abilities, they are more likely to take calculated risks, often leading to incredible achievements.

Moreover, self-confidence fosters perseverance and resilience. When faced with setbacks or failures, a self-confident individual sees these challenges as opportunities for growth instead of letting them diminish their self-worth. They will learn from their experiences and strive for improvement rather than giving up and succumbing to self-doubt.

Bernadette and Bradley continued to urge their peers to believe in themselves and foster a growth mindset. Through their experiences, they showed the importance of self-confidence in reaching one's potential, conquering fears, and achieving dreams.

So, go ahead and believe in yourself. Embrace your talents, and don't be afraid to face challenges head-on.

Remember, the journey to success begins with the first step—and that step is self-confidence.

How to Maintain Healthy Self-Confidence

Building and maintaining healthy self-confidence is super important, especially during our teenage years. It determines how we see ourselves and navigate the world around us. Luckily, there are lots of ways you can boost your self-confidence and keep it going strong. Let's get started.

- Understand your strengths and limitations: Confidence doesn't mean you have to be perfect at everything. Get in the habit of recognizing what you're good at while also acknowledging areas where you might need improvement. We all have strengths and limitations, and that's perfectly normal. Embracing these can help you feel more secure in your own skin.

- Identify what you're good at: We all have talents, so take some time to discover yours. Maybe you're an amazing artist or have a knack for making people laugh. Whatever it is, recognizing and celebrating your strengths is a key step in building a healthy self-confidence.

- Enhance your strengths: Once you've identified your strengths, focus your energy on improving and further developing them. Join clubs, take classes, or find online resources to help you hone your skills. As you become even better at your talents, your confidence will grow too.

- Be kind to yourself and others: It's easy to be hard on ourselves, especially when we're teens. But instead of putting yourself down, try treating yourself with kindness, understanding, and encouragement. Remember to celebrate your successes and forgive yourself when you make mistakes and do the same to others. Through kindness and understanding, you'll become acceptant of allowing yourself to learn from your past experiences. After all, nobody's perfect.

- Be active: Exercise can boost your mood, help you feel good about your body, and provide a sense of accomplishment. So, make time for your favorite sport, take a dance class, or simply go for a walk with friends. Your self-confidence will thank you.

- Be patient: Building self-confidence won't happen overnight, and that's okay. Like any good thing, it takes time and effort. Be patient with yourself as you work on your self-confidence and remember that even small progress is still progress.

- Surround yourself with positivity: Friends, family, and even the media you consume can have an enormous impact on your self-confidence. Make sure to surround yourself with positive people who support and uplift you and take a break from or limit the time spent with negative influences. Consuming positive and motivational content can also reinforce your confidence-building efforts.

- Learn from setbacks: We all face setbacks and challenges in our lives. But instead of dwelling on them, try to see each one as an opportunity to learn and grow. By reframing setbacks as growth experiences, you'll feel more equipped to tackle future challenges with confidence.

While building your self-confidence can seem like a daunting task, with these practical steps in hand, you'll be able to build your momentum. Remember to be patient, kind, and persistent with yourself as you embark on this journey toward a more confident and brighter future. As you grow into a confident teen, you'll unlock new opportunities, form stronger relationships, and be able to face life's challenges head-on. So go on and confidently conquer the world.

You Are Enough

Navigating the ups and downs of teenage years can be a challenging experience. There's often immense pressure to fit in, excel academically, and make big decisions about your future—all while trying to figure out who you are and your place in the world. Amidst all this, you may sometimes feel overwhelmed, inadequate, or compare yourself to others more than you should. However, no matter what you go through, you are enough.

Acknowledging that you are enough means accepting and embracing the fact that you are a work in progress. You don't have to be perfect, and nobody expects you to be. You're allowed to make mistakes as long as you learn from them and grow in the process. It's always better to try, to stumble, and to learn than to hold yourself back out of fear of failure. After all, it's the failures that often shape us and teach us the most valuable lessons in life.

Comparing yourself to others is normal, but it's crucial not to let it consume you. We live in a world that's increasingly connected and packed with images of people who seem to have it all figured out. It's easy to get caught up in wanting to be like them, but it's crucial to remember that what you see on the surface rarely reflects other people's true struggles and insecurities. You are enough just as you are, with your unique strengths, talents, dreams, and quirks.

Everyone has their individual story to tell; the path to success is different for everyone, and comparing yourself to others will only hold you back. Instead, focus on your own journey and appreciate the small victories along the way. To truly believe that you are enough means accepting and loving yourself, curating your unique personality and skill set.

It's also essential to stay in close contact with people who support and encourage your growth. Positive relationships can help you foster a healthy self-image and inspire you to embark on recent adventures with confidence, knowing that you are enough to face whatever challenges may come your way.

Moreover, practicing self-compassion is an invaluable skill as you navigate your life, as it allows you to cultivate a kinder relationship with yourself. When you embrace self-compassion, you'll find that it's easier to forgive yourself for your mistakes, accept your imperfections, and, ultimately, understand that you are worthy of love and belonging, just as you are.

In conclusion, remember that being a teen comes with its challenges, but it's an incredibly transformative and formative phase of life. You're going to make mistakes, experience setbacks, and face moments of self-doubt. But with every experience, embrace the knowledge that you are enough, for you are a unique and evolving individual who is continuously growing and learning.

Hold on to that belief, carry it with you, and see how your world will change for the better.

Reflection Questions

Do you have a healthy level of self-confidence?

_____

_____

_____

_____

_____

_____

_____

What can you do to improve your self-confidence?

_____

_____

_____

_____

_____

_____

_____

_____

What do you believe are the most important aspects of a positive self-image?

_____

_____

_____

_____

_____

_____

_____

_____

How can you practice self-compassion if you're struggling with negative thoughts about yourself?

_____

_____

_____

174

_____

_____

_____

_____

_____

What relationships have been most influential in helping you foster a healthy self-image?

_____

_____

_____

_____

_____

_____

_____

_____

What can you do to celebrate your successes and achievements, both big and small?

_____

_____

_____

_____

_____

_____

_____

_____

How has (or can) believing that "you are enough"
changed your life?

_____

_____

_____

_____

_____

_____

_____

_____

Chapter 12:

Social Media and Frenemies

One warm summer afternoon, long-time teenage friends Bernadette and Bradley were hanging out at the local ice cream parlor after school. As they savored their double-chocolate ice cream cones, they couldn't help but notice how the other kids in their hangout spot were so absorbed in their phones, hardly acknowledging each other. They knew social media influenced their teenage lives, but they were questioning the potentially negative impact of its excessive use.

Bradley recounted to Bernadette how, earlier this week, he had noticed a sharp divide between two groups in school caused by a contentious online debate. The disagreement over a famous YouTuber's performance had spiraled out of control and led to hurtful comments and personal jabs. Caught up in the whirlwind of likes, shares, and comments, both sides were blinded to how cruel their words had become.

Bernadette agreed and shared her recent experience of feeling overwhelmed trying to keep up with a constant stream of updates and notifications on her various social media accounts. She felt pressured to respond to every message and comment, but the constant bombardment had left her exhausted, anxious, and unable to focus on her studies or hobbies. She also felt inferior when comparing herself to others online, believing that their perfect lives must mean that she was lacking in some way.

As their conversation continued, Bernadette and Bradley realized that excessive social media use could negatively impact their mental health, with feelings of fear of missing out (FOMO) and constant comparison fueling anxiety and depression. They understood certain platforms could foster superficial connections without leaving much room for deep, meaningful conversations or experiences.

Moreover, they knew that it was crucial to remember people only curated their best moments on their profiles, glossing over the mundane, ordinary parts of life. They acknowledged that chasing after arbitrary goals like a certain number of likes, followers, or comments could lead to a perpetual state of dissatisfaction and distraction from what truly mattered in life.

178

Bradley and Bernadette agreed to commit to being more mindful of their social media habits—to engage only in positive and meaningful interactions and remind each other to take breaks or step back from their online presence.

With their renewed understanding, Bernadette and Bradley spent the rest of their summer exploring local parks, picking up cycling together, and visiting their favorite ice cream parlor. They would document their memories, but not at the expense of fully living in the moment.

As Bernadette and Bradley learned, it is essential for teenagers to remember that while social media can indeed have its benefits, it is vital to strike a healthy balance and not let it consume your entire life. Prioritizing real, face-to-face connections and pursuing personal growth and development outside the virtual world can lead to a happier, more fulfilling life.

Social Media and Your Learning Ability

Social media has become an integral part of our daily lives, influencing everything from communication to entertainment. For today's generation, it is a constant, ever-present force that shapes the way we interact with the world. But what impact does social media have on our learning ability?

Platforms such as Instagram, TikTok, Snapchat, and Facebook are brimming with content that often amounts to mere noise—material that does not necessarily contribute to our knowledge or personal growth. While it's true that social media has revolutionized how we communicate and access information, it also exposes us to a vast amount of low-quality, irrelevant, or even fake data.

One issue arising from your constant exposure to social media is the gradual shortening of your attention span. When you scroll down our Instagram or TikTok feeds, you are exposed to a ceaseless flow of ever-changing images, videos, and ideas. As your brain grows accustomed to this rapid pace of information consumption, your ability to maintain a focus on more detailed, longer pieces of information diminishes (Reed, 2022).

This change in your attention span can have detrimental effects on your learning ability, especially for you, a teen who is still developing your cognitive skills. The inability to concentrate on tasks for extended periods can hinder the absorption of more complex ideas and information, leading to reduced academic performance and a lack of thorough understanding of essential concepts (Reed, 2022).

Besides affecting your attention span, social media can also impact your critical thinking abilities. By nature, these platforms prioritize content that is quick, catchy, and easily digestible. This encourages users to consume information on a superficial level rather than diving deep into subjects and thinking critically about their validity and relevance (Rawat, 2021).

It's crucial to find a balance between the entertainment that social media offers and the need for focused, disciplined learning. Effective time management techniques, such as allocating specific periods for academic work or reading, can help create a more balanced lifestyle.

Why Is Balance Important with Social Media Usage?

While social media might be fun and entertaining at times, it has more drawbacks than you might realize. Here are a few examples of why it's important to monitor your usage:

- Mental health: Studies have shown that excessive social media use can lead to negative feelings such as anxiety, depression, low self-esteem, and FOMO (Albano, 2021). Being aware and proactive about your habits can help maintain a healthy mindset.

- Sleep quality: Spending too much time on screens, especially before bedtime, disrupts your sleep schedule and affects your overall well-being. Understanding your usage habits helps you create a healthy balance between screen time and rest (Kirkman, 2020).

- School success: Ensuring healthy boundaries between online activities and schoolwork will improve your academic performance.

- Privacy and safety: By monitoring and adjusting privacy settings on social media platforms, you're protecting yourself from online threats or cyberbullying and keeping personal information safe (Kirkman, 2020).

- Building a positive digital footprint: Understanding the impacts of your online activities and maintaining a responsible, respectful social media presence is essential for your reputation and future.

Social Media and Your Relationships

Social media has drastically changed the way people interact in relationships. It has become an easy way for teens to stay connected with friends and family, share their thoughts and feelings, and create meaningful bonds. However, social media can also have a negative impact on relationships if not used responsibly.

With the ability to quickly connect directly with someone through messages or posts, there is a potential to cause hurtful misunderstandings in relationships. When disagreements arise, it can be difficult to properly express yourself accurately through typed words without the benefit of body language or eye contact. This can easily lead to miscommunication and hurtful comments that are taken out of context.

Another issue is that social media can take away from quality time spent together in person with friends and family. Without meaningful face-to-face interactions, relationships may become strained as communication becomes more distant and lacking in depth.

Remember—even though technology makes it easier than ever before to keep in touch with people from around the world, having healthy relationships requires real human interaction where you can talk openly and honestly about your feelings. Social media should be seen as a tool for augmenting existing relationships rather than replacing them with virtual ones.

Cyberbullying

In today's world of social media, it's essential to understand certain concepts like cyberbullying and frenemies so you can have a great and safe online experience. Let's dive into what these terms mean and why it's crucial for you to recognize them.

Cyberbullying refers to the act of using digital platforms, like social media, to harass, threaten, embarrass, or target someone intentionally and repeatedly (Vogels, 2022). It's like regular bullying but takes place online, making it even more harmful because the bullies can hide behind a screen and sometimes remain anonymous.

Some different types of cyberbullying are:

- Flaming: When someone uses harsh language or insults to provoke a fight online.

- Harassing: Repeatedly sending harmful or offensive messages.

- Outing: Publicly sharing someone's private or embarrassing information without their consent.

- Exclusion: Deliberately ignoring or excluding someone from online group activities.

- Impersonation: Pretending to be someone else online to portray them negatively or share false information (Securly, 2018).

Understanding this is essential because cyberbullying can cause severe emotional distress and affect both the victims and the bullies themselves. It can lead to anxiety, depression, and in some cases, even self-harm or suicide. It's vital to recognize the signs and instances of cyberbullying and report it to adults or take appropriate steps to stop it.

Frenemies

A "frenemy" is a combination of "friend" and "enemy," meaning someone who pretends to be a friend but isn't genuine. Frenemies might act kind and interested in you, but secretly, they might be jealous or have ulterior motives. They can contribute to a toxic environment, and their actions can be harmful to your mental and emotional well-being (Maxabella, 2020).

Some indicators that you might have frenemies:

- They often criticize or put you down.

- They seem happy when you face challenges or fail.

- They compete with you rather than support you.

- They might spread rumors or gossip about you behind your back.

- They aren't there for you when you need them most.

Recognizing frenemies is crucial because having them in your social circles can lead to self-doubt, loneliness, and a sense of betrayal. Identifying them allows you to reevaluate your relationships and redirect your focus to people who genuinely support and care for you.

Now that you know what cyberbullying and frenemies are, you can better comprehend the potential difficulties that you might face on social media. This knowledge allows you to protect yourself, take appropriate action, and maintain a positive and healthy online experience. Remember to always treat others with kindness and empathy while navigating the digital world.

Real vs. Reel

Real vs. reel is a concept that teens should understand when using the online world and social media, especially in terms of what they are sharing about themselves with others. Real is referring to "real life"—it's the way things actually are, not how they may appear online. Reel can be thought of as a "virtual world" or the image that one wants to portray on social media and other digital platforms—this can often look much different from who someone really is (Watkins, 2017).

Understanding what is "real" versus what is "reel," is important because you need to know that what people share online does not necessarily reflect who they really are in "real life"—even if people may perceive it as such. Remember that what you post on social media can have lasting effects, both good and bad, so you must consider all aspects before you post anything.

You should also know many other users don't always tell the truth in their posts, so you should take any claims with a grain of salt. You should know the potential dangers of being overly reliant on digital connections instead of face-to-face interactions, such as feeling depressed, isolated, or generally unwell.

In short, understanding real vs. reel isn't just about making sure your online persona reflects your true identity; it's also about recognizing that digital technology has its limits and recognizing when to turn off your devices and spend quality time with friends and family in person.

Protecting Yourself Online

In today's digital world, protecting yourself online is more important than ever. As technology continues to advance, new dangers emerge that teenagers need to be aware of. While the Internet can be a fantastic tool for learning, connecting, and having fun, it can also be a breeding ground for predators and cyberbullying.

Teens are more susceptible to dangers online because they often have less experience with technology and are more trusting. Furthermore, teenagers frequently share personal information online without understanding the potential consequences. This puts them at a higher risk of falling victim to cyberbullying, identity theft, and online predators (Ben-Joseph, 2018). Learning to protect yourself online is essential for everyone, but it is especially crucial for young people who may not have fully developed critical thinking and decision-making skills.

The Internet is an incredible tool that allows us to communicate, share information, and access a world of knowledge. However, it also poses some risks that must be taken seriously. Here are some tips on how teens can stay safe online:

- Be aware of what you post and whom you interact with: Be mindful of the information you share online. Post only things that are appropriate, and don't give out personal information such as your address or phone number to anyone you do not know well.

Additionally, be aware of whom you are interacting with online, as they may not have your best interest at heart.

- You should also consider limiting virtual interactions and prioritize face-to-face communication. It is essential to find a balance between virtual and in-person interactions. Too much time spent online can lead to issues such as social isolation and the development of unhealthy relationships. It can be easier for people to misrepresent themselves or their intentions online, leading to potential misunderstandings, hurt feelings, or even dangerous situations.

- Set up strong passwords: It is essential to use strong passwords when creating accounts or logging in to websites or apps. Use a combination of letters, numbers, symbols, and capital letters for extra security. Avoid using the same password for each account and change them regularly.

- Practice good cyber hygiene: Keep your computer and other devices up-to-date with the latest antivirus software so you can prevent malicious activities from occurring on your computer system. Also, if using public Wi-Fi networks, make sure the network is encrypted so no one can track what websites you visit or view any personal information that is sent through the connection.

- Think before clicking links: Links can lead to malicious web pages designed to steal personal information or infect devices with malware and viruses, so be cautious before clicking links sent via email or posted on social media platforms. Make sure they are from a trusted source before accessing them, as they could contain malicious content even if they look legitimate at first glance.

- Be cautious when playing online games: Playing online games can be a fun way to connect with others, but it can also present risks. Be careful when interacting with strangers online, and avoid sharing personal information with them. Remember that people might not always be who they claim to be, and a friendly face can sometimes hide a sinister motive.

Monitoring and Improving Your Usage

As a teen in the digital age, you probably enjoy the perks of social media and being connected with friends, family, and the world. However, it is essential to consider your online and social media usage deliberately. Monitoring and improving your online habits will keep you safe, protect your mental health, and allow you to use social media as a beneficial tool.

Here's a simple guide on how to monitor and improve your social media habits:

- Track your time: Keep tabs on how long you spend online or using social media. Use built-in smartphone features like Screen Time on iPhones or Digital Wellbeing on Android devices to monitor your app usage. Take note of any patterns, like spending too much time on a particular app or becoming distracted during important tasks.

- Set daily or weekly limits: Now that you have tracked your social media usage, set realistic time limits for each app. Use those same monitoring tools to set app time limits and adhere to those limits every day. This helps you stay in control of your time and prevents mindless scrolling.

- Minimize multitasking: According to experts, multitasking and switching between apps can decrease your productivity and hinder your ability to focus. To improve your online usage, give your full attention to one task or app at a time.

- Prioritize quality content: When creating and maintaining your account, fill your social media feeds with content and accounts that inspire, educate, and make you feel good. Regularly review who you're following and unfollow accounts that make you feel anxious or insecure.

- Turn off unnecessary notifications: Excessive notifications can lead to increased phone usage and distractions. Disable nonessential notifications to reduce compulsive checking of social media.

- Keep the Internet as a tool: Focus on building strong, in-person relationships and using the Internet primarily as a learning tool or for occasional entertainment. Remember that authentic connections often grow from face-to-face interactions, which provide valuable opportunities to build trust and communication skills.

- Regular check-ins: Evaluate your social media habits and feelings to make necessary adjustments. Are you satisfied with the time spent on these apps? Do your chosen platforms contribute positively to your life?

Reflection Questions

Do you spend a lot of time on social media? If so, how do you think it affects you?

_____

_____

_____

_____

_____

_____

_____

_____

Can you draw the connection between a time you felt sad or angry looking at social media? On the opposite side, can you think of a time that social media made you happy or excited?

_____

_____

_____

_____

_____

_____

_____

Are you conscious of your online privacy?

_____

_____

_____

_____

_____

_____

_____

How can you improve your online habits and ensure your privacy is protected?

_____

_____

_____

_____

_____

_____

_____

In what ways do you think understanding the concept of real vs. reel can help with making better decisions regarding online and social media usage?

_____

_____

_____

_____

_____

_____

What strategies have you implemented to monitor and control your online and social media usage?

What tips do you have for others on how to maintain a healthy balance between the real world and the virtual world?

How do you think monitoring and controlling your online and social media usage can help build a positive digital footprint?

If you could change one thing about social media, what would it be?

Chapter 13:

Belonging and Peer Pressure

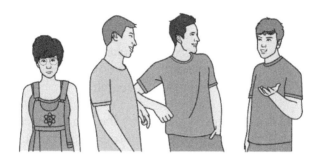

On one of the last days of summer, Bernadette was sitting in her room thinking about how summer was ending, and school was just around the corner. Her best friend, Bradley, popped up in her mind, and she thought about how they had shared laughter and tears and celebrated small victories together since elementary school.

A few days before the start of school year, Bernadette was thrilled to receive an invitation to the most sought-after end of summer party from a classmate. Without a second thought, she asked Bradley to come along. That fateful night, while they were having a great time, someone brought out a pack of cigarettes, and the cool kids at the party started urging Bernadette to take a puff.

Despite her hesitance, they made a compelling case about how gratifying it feels and assured her that just one try would change her life. Bernadette didn't want a cigarette, but she desperately wanted to fit in with the cool kids, so she hesitated.

This is when Bradley could see the dilemma on her face and stepped in to help. He reminded Bernadette how they had been supporting each other through thick and thin and that they had their own unique qualities that made them who they were. He took her aside and explained how peer pressure could sometimes make people do things they wouldn't have done otherwise and that it's important to stay true to oneself.

As Bernadette listened to Bradley, she began to realize how her decision might affect their friendship, her future aspirations, and her health. She decided to stand her ground and politely declined the offer to smoke.

In the days that followed, Bernadette understood that learning to handle peer pressure effectively was crucial for her personal growth and mental well-being. She learned to prioritize her values and goals over fitting in with others. Instead of focusing on fitting in with the popular crowd, she focused on building stronger relationships with her true friends, who accepted her for who she was.

Meanwhile, Bradley continued to stand firm in his beliefs, proudly representing his unique identity and encouraging Bernadette to do the same. During their time in high school, they both faced different kinds of peer pressure, but they dealt with it efficiently, side by side.

This story spread among other students, and both Bernadette and Bradley became role models for others in their school to deal with peer pressure, due to their courage handling this situation gracefully. Their story teaches us that it is okay to say no to things that don't align with our values and the importance of having supportive friends who love and respect us for who we are.

The lesson here is that, in our lives, we will encounter situations where we may feel the pressure to conform to the expectations of others. It is essential to recognize the importance of standing up for what we believe is right, even when it is difficult, and that true friends will accept us for who we are.

By learning from the example set by Bernadette and Bradley, we can become better equipped to handle peer pressure and stay true to ourselves in our journey through life.

What Is Belonging and How Can It Lead to Peer Pressure

Belonging is about feeling connected with a group of people or a community. It's the sense that you are part of something bigger than yourself and have an important role to play. When we feel like we belong, we tend to be more confident and open to new experiences.

Needing to belong is a normal human desire that starts when we're young and continues throughout our lives. This need can create pressure for teenagers in particular, as they often want to be accepted by their peers or "fit in" with their social group. As a result, teens may put up with peer pressure in order to maintain or increase their sense of belonging within the group (McDonald, 2018).

Peer pressure can also lead teens to take part in activities they wouldn't otherwise do, such as drinking alcohol or smoking cigarettes, because they want acceptance from their peers. While these behaviors may make them feel included in the moment, it can lead to problems down the road if not handled properly (McDonald, 2018). Teenagers should remember that true friends won't make them do something that will hurt them physically or emotionally; if this happens, it's time for some new friends!

Overall, the need for belonging is an important component of any teen's life, but friendships should always be based on mutual respect and safety. Trying too hard to fit in might cause more harm than good in the long run—so be sure your choices are ones you can stand behind even if your friends aren't around!

How to Manage the Peer Pressure

The desire to belong and be part of a group is an instinct that has helped humans survive and thrive for generations. However, this evolution-driven need for social acceptance can sometimes lead to peer pressure, influencing and pressuring people, especially teens, to do things they might not be comfortable with or that go against their values.

Trust Your Instincts

If you feel uncomfortable or uneasy about a certain situation, always trust your instincts. Your intuition is usually right, and you shouldn't ignore it just to fit in with your peers. When something doesn't feel right, give yourself permission to step back and question if it aligns with your values and beliefs.

Build Self-Confidence

Developing self-confidence is a key aspect of resisting peer pressure. When you're confident in who you are and what you believe in, it becomes easier to stand up for yourself and make your own decisions. This includes finding your passions, setting goals, and focusing on personal growth.

Learn to Say No

Sometimes, the hardest part about dealing with peer pressure is simply saying no. However, stand your ground when faced with situations that make you uncomfortable. Remember that it's okay to say no, without having to give elaborate explanations or justifications for your decision.

Choose the Right Friends

Be friends with people who share similar values and interests and who respect and support your choices. Friends who consistently pressure you into making decisions you're not comfortable with might not be the best influence on your life.

Seek Positive Role Models

Look for positive role models in your life, like parents, teachers, coaches, or family friends, who can provide guidance, support, and advice on handling difficult situations. They can help you navigate and resist peer pressure and even share their own experiences with it.

Plan Ahead

It's easier to resist peer pressure when you're prepared for situations in which it might arise. Plan ahead by thinking about how you would react in these circumstances and have some responses ready. This way, you will feel less caught off-guard and more confident in your decision.

Be a Leader

Instead of always following others, strive to be a leader in your group. By leading, you can positively influence your peers and create a healthier social environment where everyone feels respected and heard. This may be challenging at first; however, practice makes perfect!

Practice Being Assertive

Learning how to be assertive is a great way to handle peer pressure. Assertiveness is a form of communication that involves clearly expressing your thoughts, feelings, and needs while respecting the rights of others. Expressing yourself in this manner will help you stand up for yourself when needed and resist peer pressure.

Ask for Help When Necessary

If you're facing serious peer pressure, don't hesitate to reach out to a trusted adult or authority figure for help. They can intervene, guide, or even get involved, if necessary, to ensure your safety and well-being.

Resisting and handling peer pressure is a vital skill in developing your own identity and making healthy, informed decisions. By understanding your values, standing up for yourself, and surrounding yourself with a supportive environment, you can successfully navigate the pressures of adolescence and emerge as a confident, independent individual.

Reflection Questions

Do you struggle to fit in with others?

_____

_____

_____

_____

_____

_____

_____

_____

Do you deal with a lot of peer pressure? If so, how does it make you feel?

Do you think you may have peer pressured someone in the past? If so, how does that make you feel?

How do you deal with peer pressure in a way that is respectful of yourself and others?

How else can you deal with peer pressure in the future?

What advice do you have for someone struggling with peer pressure?

Are there any positive aspects of peer pressure? If yes, what are they?

Chapter 14:

Love Interests

Bernadette and Bradley had been inseparable friends since their childhood days—laughing, sharing secrets, and exploring their surroundings together. As the years went by, their bond only grew stronger, weaving a unique tapestry of trust and understanding.

Bernadette, a sweet and thoughtful girl, developed a secret crush on her best friend, Bradley. However, she kept it a secret, always prioritizing their friendship over her emotions. Bradley, a friendly and artistic young man, was completely oblivious to Bernadette's feelings and suddenly found himself smitten by a new girl in town—Melinda.

One day, as they were chatting in the schoolyard, Bradley gleefully shared the news with Bernadette, his eyes sparkling with delight. "I think I'm in love with Melinda!", he exclaimed. Bernadette, masking her pain with a warm smile, helped Bradley make sense of his newfound feelings.

Taking a deep breath, Bernadette asked Bradley to describe the emotions he felt when he was around Melinda. "Well, every time I see her or talk to her, my heart races, and I feel butterflies in my stomach," Bradley explained. "I can't stop thinking about her, and it's like all the colors in the world become more vibrant when she's near."

Bernadette nodded thoughtfully and said, "That's a beautiful way to describe it, Bradley. Love is a powerful, multifaceted emotion that can encompass a variety of feelings. Sometimes, love can make you feel giddy, excited, and a little scared all at once. People often mistake infatuation or attraction for love, but true love tends to deepen over time and comes with loyalty, trust, respect, and a strong emotional and mental connection."

Bradley listened intently as Bernadette continued. "Love isn't always easy, and it can be confusing, but it's a beautiful and profound emotion. You'll continue to learn and grow as you explore this new relationship. Just remember that communication and understanding are key to a healthy and successful relationship."

Hearing Bernadette's wise words, Bradley felt grateful for their friendship and her willingness to help him understand love. "Thank you, Bernadette. You always know the right things to say, and I can't express how glad I am to have you as my friend," said Bradley, who then hugged his best friend tightly.

Secretly, Bernadette's heart ached as Bradley's words landed like heavy stones on her fragile emotions. But she knew that true love meant putting others' happiness before our own, even when it hurt us deeply. And so, Bernadette chose to be an unwavering friend, helping Bradley navigate the beautiful and treacherous journey of love.

And thus, as the seasons passed, and the stars looked upon their town with a gentle gaze, Bernadette and Bradley's story unfolded—a tale of love, friendship, pain, and understanding that would continue to echo through the pages of time teaching countless hearts the true meaning of love.

What Is Love?

Love is a complex and powerful emotion that can be described as a deep affection, care, and attachment toward someone or something. It is an innate human emotion that can manifest in different forms, such as familial love, friendship, or romantic love. For teens, experiencing romantic love for the first time can be both exciting and confusing. It is essential to understand what is considered normal and what might not be normal in love, especially during teenage years when emotions can be intense and turbulent.

Love, in its healthy form, is a normal and positive emotion. It can encourage personal growth, empathy, and emotional well-being. For teens, experiencing love can be a significant milestone in their emotional development. It helps them learn how to care for others, express and manage their emotions, and establish meaningful connections with others. A healthy, loving relationship involves trust, respect, understanding, and open communication.

However, love can also have negative effects on teens if it becomes unhealthy or crosses the boundaries of others. Signs of an unhealthy relationship may include:

- Obsession: Continuously thinking about the person with little or no control, obsessively checking their social media and losing interest in other activities.

- Codependency: Relying too heavily on the other person for emotional support, happiness, or self-worth, leading to an imbalance in the relationship.

- Jealousy and control: Excessive jealousy, suspicion, or attempts to control the other person's actions or interactions with others.

- Insecurity and low self-esteem: Constantly seeking reassurance or validation from the other person or feeling unworthy of their love.

- Pressure to engage in sexual activities: A healthy relationship should involve no form of coercion or pressure to engage in sexual activities or any other activity that may make the other uncomfortable, especially for minors.

If you are experiencing any of these signs, it is important to reach out to a parent, teacher, or trusted adult for guidance and support. Remember that a healthy and loving relationship should contribute to your well-being and happiness, not diminish it.

The Psychology and Physiology of the Romantic Feelings

So, you're experiencing those warm, fuzzy feelings for someone? It's an exciting, sometimes disorienting experience, and perfectly normal! Let's dive into the fascinating world of romantic feelings and how it affects your brain and body. We'll also share some tips on how to keep those feelings grounded in a healthy and balanced way.

Love Makes Your Brain Go "Whoa!"

When we fall in love, our brain releases a cocktail of feel-good chemicals like dopamine, oxytocin, and adrenaline. These chemicals play a key role in making us feel bonded, elated, and a bit obsessed with our new special someone. Dopamine is linked to the reward system in our brain, making us feel good when we're around our crush. Meanwhile, oxytocin creates a sense of trust and attachment between partners. Adrenaline, on the other hand, is responsible for that heart-racing excitement and nervousness that you might experience around your significant other (Walsh, 2012).

Love Can Be a Little Blind

It's true what they say, love can be blind. When we're infatuated with someone, the levels of cortisol (a stress hormone) in our brains rise, impairing our ability to think clearly and objectively about the person we're falling for. Combine that with a drop in serotonin (a hormone linked to happiness and well-being), and suddenly, you might idealize your romantic interest and put them on a pedestal (Walsh, 2012).

Love Can Even Make Your Body React in Weird Ways

Love really does affect our bodies. Some physical symptoms of romantic love might include butterflies in your stomach, racing heartbeats, sweaty palms, and a dry mouth. You may also experience changes in appetite or sleep patterns or feel more energetic or lethargic than usual.

Dealing with Romantic Feelings in a Healthy Way

Our regular emotions can already be overwhelming and difficult to manage. Unfortunately, love can be a challenging emotion to overcome. However, next are a few suggestions to help you manage your relationship and emotions in a healthy way.

Take Things Slow

Since romantic feelings can cause us to lose our objectivity, it's essential to take your time when you're in the thick of these powerful emotions. Enjoy getting to know the person, and don't rush into any heavy commitments or life changes until you're sure those feelings are based on understanding and trust, not just chemistry.

Be Mindful of Your Thoughts and Feelings

When you're overwhelmed with emotion, explore your romantic feelings in a balanced way rather than getting swept away by them too quickly. Make sure you're aware of what your heart is telling you and take the time to reflect objectively on how your emotions could impact your behavior.

Keep Your Interests and Friendships

When we fall in love, it's easy to forget about other parts of our lives. Maintain your friendships and hobbies so you don't lose yourself in the romance. Your personal growth and happiness are just as important as nurturing the relationship.

Do not Forget Self-Care

Taking care of yourself is not selfish; it's necessary. Maintain healthy habits like getting enough sleep, eating well, and staying active. Also, prioritize self-reflection and emotional health—practice mindfulness, explore your feelings, and seek support from friends, family, or even a therapist when needed.

Romantic feelings are a natural and exciting part of life. By understanding the psychology and physiology behind these feelings, you can develop the self-awareness and emotional intelligence needed to navigate the thrilling world of adolescent love healthily.

Discussing Your Feelings When You Are in Love

Falling in love can be an exciting and overwhelming experience, especially for teenagers who might be dealing with these intense feelings for the first time. It's natural to want to express your emotions to the other person, but finding the right words and approach can be tricky.

Here are some steps to help you navigate this important conversation.

- Reflect on your feelings: Before approaching the person, consider your emotions and why you want to reveal them. What is it about this person that you find so appealing? Are you looking for a deep connection or just a casual relationship? Being aware of your feelings will help you communicate them better.

- Choose an appropriate timing and location: Timing can be crucial when discussing your feelings with someone. Select a moment when both of you are relaxed and comfortable, and opt for a private setting where you won't be interrupted. Avoid bringing up the topic during moments of high stress or when the other person is preoccupied.

- Start with a casual conversation: Instead of jumping straight into talking about your feelings, ease into the discussion by engaging in a light, casual conversation. Talk about common interests or shared experiences to create a comfortable atmosphere. This way, you can gauge the person's mood and assess if it's the right time to bring up your feelings.

- Be honest and direct: When you're ready to share your feelings, be clear and honest about your emotions. Use "I" statements to express your feelings, such as "I really enjoy spending time with you" or "I find myself thinking about you often." This approach helps convey your feelings without placing pressure on the other person to reciprocate immediately.

- Listen and be patient: After sharing your feelings, give the other person time to process the information and respond. Listen carefully to what they have to say and be respectful of their feelings. They might need some time to think about what you've shared, and that's alright. The important thing is that you've taken the first step in expressing your emotions.

- Prepare for different outcomes: While it would be ideal for the person, you're in love with to feel the same way, it would be ideal to prepare for various outcomes. If they don't reciprocate your feelings, it might be disappointing, but remember that it's a part of life. Know that it's better to be honest about your emotions than to keep them bottled up, and it's an opportunity for growth and self-discovery.

- Be respectful and understanding: Regardless of the outcome, it's crucial to treat the other person with respect and understanding. Thank them for listening and for any honesty they've provided in their response. Keep in mind that sometimes relationships take time to develop or aren't meant to be, which is okay.

By following these steps, you can approach and discuss your feelings with others in a respectful and honest manner. While it may seem daunting, being truthful about your emotions is an essential part of building strong relationships and deepening connections. No matter the outcome, you can grow and learn from the experience.

Building Healthy Relationships

As teenagers, there is so much to learn about the world of relationships and dating. A solid foundation of knowledge and good habits will help you navigate the turbulent waters of teenage relationships. Next, we will discuss the best five ways to build a healthy relationship.

Communication: A Key to a Successful Relationship

Communication is key in understanding and navigating the complexities of love. By talking openly with someone you trust, you can gain insight into your feelings and experiences. Sharing personal stories and learning from the experiences of others can help you better understand your emotions and make informed decisions regarding love and relationships.

Be open and share your thoughts and emotions with the person you're interested in, and encourage the other person to do the same. By being honest about your feelings, you can build a foundation of trust and understanding, which will help you navigate the ups and downs of romance.

Trust: With Confidence Comes Comfort

Trust is vital in any healthy relationship. Have faith in your partner to make good decisions, respect your feelings, and remain loyal. Moreover, be trustworthy yourself by keeping your promises, being open and honest, and respecting your partner's privacy. Trust takes time to build but can greatly strengthen your relationship.

Support: A Pillar of Strength for Each Other

Being supportive means being there for each other during both good and bad times. Encourage and uplift your partner when they need it and rejoice with them during their successes. Learning to lean on each other will create a bond that keeps your relationship strong, even during difficult times.

Equality: A Partnership

Healthy relationships consist of two individuals who treat each other with equal respect and consideration. Share responsibilities, decision-making, emotional needs, and support with your partner. Be open to compromise and negotiation, and value your partner's opinions and feelings as much as your own.

Personal Boundaries: Maintain Your Individuality

Even in a close relationship, personal boundaries are crucial. Respect your partner's need for their own space and interests while also maintaining your own hobbies, friendships, and goals. Being in a relationship shouldn't mean losing your own identity or sacrificing your personal growth.

How to Handle Unreciprocated Interest

When you're a teenager, navigating the world of crushes, dating, and relationships can be quite a rollercoaster ride. It's an exciting time, but it can also be filled with confusing emotions and tricky situations, especially when someone is interested in you—and you just don't feel the same way. Don't worry, you're not alone! Learning how to deal with this delicate situation can help you maintain your friendships and avoid hurt feelings. Just remember don't wait too long to clarify the situation, as the longer the wait is, it will get harder to handle. Here are a few steps you can take.

Step 1: Reflect on Your Feelings

Before diving into a conversation, consider how you truly feel. It's normal to feel flattered, but that doesn't mean you have to reciprocate those feelings. Be honest with yourself and consider if you could ever see yourself developing feelings for this person. If the answer is no, address the situation politely and responsibly.

Step 2: Be Approachable and Empathetic

Whether the person confesses their interest in person or through a message, it's crucial to be approachable and kind. Remember, it takes a lot of courage to be vulnerable and express feelings for another person. Imagine how you would feel if the roles were reversed. Keep this in mind and approach the conversation with sensitivity and empathy.

Step 3: Be Clear and Direct

When addressing the situation, it's vital to be honest and clear with your feelings. Using phrases like, "I appreciate your honesty, and it was brave of you to tell me, but I don't share the same feelings. I really value our friendship and hope we can continue to be friends," can demonstrate understanding while establishing boundaries. Avoid using clichés like, "You're like a sibling to me," or "It's not you, it's me." These statements can come across as insincere and leave the other person feeling even more confused.

Step 4: Be Prepared for Their Reaction

When the time comes, understand that the person might initially experience a range of emotions, from sadness to anger. Remember, they've opened themselves up to vulnerability, and rejection can be challenging to accept. Offer them support and reassurance by acknowledging their feelings and giving them space if they need it. It might be a good idea to reach out after a few days to make sure they're okay and reiterate your wish to remain friends.

Step 5: Maintain Boundaries

After you've expressed your feelings, establish and maintain boundaries to ensure a healthy friendship. This might involve avoiding certain behaviors that might make the other person feel uncomfortable, like excessive flirting or physical touch. Respect their feelings by giving them time to heal and process the situation.

Dealing with someone who's interested in you and not reciprocating their feelings can be a challenging and delicate situation. By being empathetic, direct, and respectful, you can navigate this experience while maintaining strong friendships. Remember to be honest with yourself, communicate openly, and maintain healthy boundaries as you tackle the exciting world of teenage relationships.

Standing Your Ground and Setting Boundaries in Love

Love and relationships can be an exciting and sometimes confusing part of life, but knowing how to stay true to yourself and setting boundaries creates a solid foundation to grow on. By understanding your own needs and respecting the needs of others, you can navigate these experiences with confidence and grace.

- Know your values and stick to them: First and foremost, know what is important to you, such as your beliefs, morals, and priorities. Take time to figure these out so that when you are in a relationship or dealing with love, you'll know where you stand. This can help you make informed decisions and stay true to yourself and others.

- Practice assertive communication: Being assertive doesn't mean being aggressive. It means communicating your feelings, needs, and boundaries clearly and respectfully. This might require some practice, but the more you do it, the easier it becomes. For example, you can say, "I really like spending time with you, but I need some alone time to recharge."

- Respect other people's boundaries: Just as you want others to listen to and respect your boundaries, you should do the same for them. If someone tells you they're not comfortable with a particular activity or conversation, accept it without pressuring or questioning them.

- Trust your feelings: If something doesn't feel right or you're uncomfortable with a situation, trust your gut! Give yourself permission to say "no" and stand your ground. Remember, you don't need to justify your feelings to anyone.

- Be prepared to walk away: In some cases, asserting your boundaries and staying true to yourself might mean ending a relationship or friendship. In the end, do what's best for you, even if it's difficult or painful in the short term.

- Give and receive love with self-respect: Remember that you deserve love, respect, and kindness. Don't let anyone make you feel otherwise. Likewise, show respect and love to others without compromising your own values and boundaries.

- Consider your emotional, physical, and digital boundaries: Boundaries aren't just about physical touch or personal space. Don't forget to set emotional and digital boundaries too. This can include how much time you spend together, how often you text, and what you share online.

- Make self-care a priority: You are your first priority. Take care of yourself, both physically and emotionally. Taking time to recharge and practicing self-compassion can help you recognize your needs and set healthy boundaries.

- Remember, "no" is a complete sentence: You don't always need to explain your boundaries to others. Sometimes, a simple "no" is enough to communicate your feelings and stand your ground.

- Keep re-evaluating boundaries: As you grow and change, your boundaries might evolve too. Have personal check-ins with yourself regularly and reassess your boundaries to make sure they still feel right to you.

Remember, it's perfectly okay to stand your ground and protect your personal boundaries, even when in love. It's a sign of respect and maturity to recognize your own limitations and communicate them honestly with others. So don't be afraid to say no, even in the most emotionally charged situations.

How to Bounce Back from Rejection

Let's face it, rejection is a part of life, and it's absolutely natural to feel hurt or upset when someone isn't interested in you. Whether it's being turned down for a date, being ignored by a crush, or simply not being included in a group of friends, rejection can sting. But fear not, because we are here with some tips and advice that can help you deal with rejection and come out even stronger!

Give Yourself Permission to Feel Disappointed

Rejection can hurt, and that's completely normal! Let yourself feel the emotions that come with being rejected rather than suppressing them. Acknowledge and accept your feelings, allow yourself some time to be upset, and then gradually shift your focus to more positive thoughts.

Getting Rejected Happens to Anyone

Remind yourself that even the most popular and successful people experience rejection. It is a common and unavoidable part of life. Just because you may have been rejected in one particular situation, it doesn't mean that you're a failure or unworthy of great relationships and experiences in the future. Remember, everyone goes through this at some point, and it's totally normal.

Practice Self-Compassion and Self-Love

In the face of rejection, it's easy to start questioning your self-worth and fall into a spiral of negative self-talk. To combat this, be kind to yourself and practice self-compassion. Treat yourself like you would a good friend who is going through the same thing—with love, understanding, and support. Focus on your strengths, celebrate your achievements, and remind yourself of your value.

Contact Supportive People

Reach out to your friends and family members for support and share your feelings with them. Being around people who love and care for you can help you recover from rejection much more quickly. They can be a source of encouragement and advice and can provide you with a new perspective on the situation.

Keep Things in Perspective

It's essential not to let a single rejection define your entire self-worth or future success. Remind yourself that one person's opinion or preferences do not represent how everyone sees you. Keep in mind that people's choices are influenced by many factors, many of which have nothing to do with your qualities.

Learn From the Experience

Taking the time to reflect on the situation can help you learn and grow from it. Ask yourself if there's anything you could have done differently or if there were any signals that you might have missed. The key is not to dwell on the negative aspects of the experience but to use it as an opportunity to learn and become better in future situations.

Stay Focused on Your Goals and Interests

Instead of being consumed by the feeling of rejection, channel your energy into doing the things you love and pursuing your passions. Engage in activities that make you happy, join clubs or organizations where you can meet like-minded people, and continue to work on your own personal growth.

Time Heals Wounds and Things Will Get Better

Rejection may feel like the end of the world right now, but remember that this too shall pass. As time goes on, the sting of rejection will naturally subside, and you will regain your confidence and strength. In the meantime, be patient and kind to yourself—you're stronger than you think!

Dealing with rejection might seem daunting, but with the right mindset and support system, you can bounce back and emerge as a stronger, more resilient person. Remember, every experience, good or bad, helps shape us into the unique and amazing individuals we are. Keep moving forward, and never let rejection hold you back from living your best life!

Getting Sexually Active

Getting sexually active is a normal and natural part of growing up for many people. It can be a pleasurable experience that allows you to explore your feelings, deepen your relationship with someone, and learn more about your own body. However, as fun, and pleasurable as being intimate may be, it is important to remember that it also comes with major adult-like responsibilities and potential risks, especially if you start at a young age and too early.

First, let's understand that intimacy can have many positive aspects. It can bring two people closer together, fostering trust, communication, and love. Physical touch and closeness can also release "feel-good" hormones, such as oxytocin and endorphins, increasing positive feelings and well-being.

A crucial consideration to make when becoming sexually active is the risk of contracting sexually transmitted diseases (STDs). STDs are infections that are spread through sexual contact, and they can have serious and irreversible health consequences if left untreated. Some common STDs include chlamydia, gonorrhea, and human papillomavirus (HPV). HIV and hepatitis b and c are also among life threatening STD infections. To reduce the risk of contracting an STD, it is crucial to practice safe sex by using condoms and getting regularly tested.

Another key responsibility associated with sexual activity is the potential for unplanned pregnancy. Contraceptive methods such as birth control pills, intrauterine devices (IUDs), and condoms can greatly reduce the risk of an unintended pregnancy. However, no method is 100% foolproof, so it is essential to be aware of the consequences and be prepared to handle them responsibly.

Engaging in sexual activity at a young age can have a significant impact on your life path and goals. For example, an unplanned pregnancy might require you to rearrange your priorities and make sacrifices that could affect your education, career, and overall future. The emotional consequences of being sexually active can be challenging, as relationships might become more complicated, and your feelings and self-esteem could be affected.

Keep in mind that this time and experiences in your life are unique and precious moments, and you will never get to experience them again. Focusing too much on adult-like activities might detract from your ability to fully enjoy and take advantage of your youth. Instead, use this time to discover your passions, work toward your goals, and build sound foundations for your future.

In the end, before getting involved in intimate relationships, make sure you are well informed about the consequences and are prepared to handle them maturely. Ensure that you are practicing safe sex, using contraception to prevent unplanned pregnancies, and prioritizing your long-term goals and well-being. And always remember there is no rush to grow up—enjoy your teenage years while they last!

The Four Principles of Sexual Consent

Now that we have discussed the ways to build a healthy relationship, let's dive into an equally important topic: sexual consent. The four principles of sexual consent are:

Freely Given: Consent Must Be Voluntary

Consent should be given without any form of pressure, manipulation, or coercion. Both you and your partner should feel entirely comfortable and want to engage in contact of any sort.

Reversible: You Can Change Your Mind

At any point, either you or your partner can change your mind and withdraw consent. Be aware of your partner's feelings and respect their decision if they decide they are uncomfortable or do not want to continue.

Informed: Knowledge Is Power

You and your partner must understand the risks involved and share your intentions and boundaries before participating in any sexual activities. Having a clear understanding of what you both consent to will ensure a safer and more enjoyable experience.

Specific: Clear Consent for Every Activity

Asking for and giving consent should be specific to each sexual activity you engage in with your partner. Just because someone agrees to one action does not mean they agree to all sexual activities. Keep the communication open and ask for consent at every step.

Reflection Questions

Have you experienced love yet? If so, do you think it was healthy?

How do you know if someone likes you or is interested in you?

_____

_____

_____

_____

_____

_____

_____

_____

How do you know if you like someone?

_____

_____

_____

_____

_____

_____

_____

_____

How do you tell or show someone you're interested in them?

_____

_____

_____

_____

_____

_____

_____

_____

What can you do to improve communication in your relationships?

_____

_____

_____

_____

_____

_____

_____

235

How can you create a safe and trusting environment with your partner?

Have you been rejected before? How did you feel?

Have you had to reject someone else's feelings before? How did you feel and how do you think the other person took it?

What would you do to prepare if you decide to be sexually active? What would you do to prepare if you decide to be sexually active? What is the right age to be sexually active in your opinion?

Do you know how to set healthy boundaries?

How do you communicate your needs and boundaries to your partner?

_____

_____

_____

What do you think makes a relationship strong and successful?

_____

_____

_____

_____

_____

_____

_____

Chapter 15:

Financing and Spending

Bernadette and Bradley were planning to go to the same college after high school, and they had already thought about what their lives would be like in just a few short months.

One day, Bernadette mentioned to Bradley that she was worried about how she could afford college tuition. As it turned out, she has already spent a good chunk of the money that her family had saved up to cover the cost of college, and she would need to find a way to make up the difference now. She exclaimed in frustration: "Brad, I don't even remember how I have used up that much money?!"

Bradley tried his best to help comfort Bernadette with kind words and encouragement, but he realized he needed to provide her with more substantial advice. He told her that she can't reverse what is done already, but managing finances during college would be even more essential if she wanted to succeed academically and still have time for fun activities, without worrying to run out of money.

He explained that budgeting is a key skill set to master because through proper budgeting one can manage their spending so they could have enough money for rent, food, books, and other necessities while still being able to do some extra things like going out with friends or buying something they wanted every now and again. He also pointed out that having an emergency fund is important so there's always a safety net in case anything unexpected comes up financially.

The importance of understanding finances for teens cannot be overstated; knowing how to manage your money will enable you to live comfortably throughout your years in college without compromising your academic success or social life.

Basics of Finances for Teens

Understanding finances might seem like a daunting task, but it is actually quite simple when broken down. Here

242

are some essential basics of finances for you, helping you become a responsible and money-savvy teen. Ready to level up your financial game?

Know the Difference Between Needs and Wants

An important lesson in financial literacy is distinguishing between your needs and wants. Needs are essential items that you can't live without—like food, shelter, and clothing. Wants are things you'd like to have but can live without—like that new pair of shoes or a shiny new gadget.

Before you spend your hard-earned cash, ask yourself: "Is this item really necessary for my survival or well-being?" Making wise purchasing decisions and prioritizing needs over wants can help you save money and avoid financial pitfalls.

Set a Realistic Budget

A budget is a plan that outlines your income (money you receive) and expenses (money you spend). Creating a budget can help you keep track of your spending habits and ensure you're not overspending.

Start by noting down your monthly income—this could be an allowance from your parents, the money you earn from a part-time job, or even small side hustles like babysitting or selling handmade crafts.

Next, list down your monthly expenses—these will mostly be needs like food, transportation, and school-related costs. Don't forget to allot some money for personal savings and entertainment (you deserve some fun, too!).

Subtract your expenses from your income and see how much money you have left at the end of the month. Adjust your expenses accordingly to ensure that you're always living within your means.

Save Money for Future Goals and Emergencies

As the famous saying goes, "A penny saved is a penny earned." It's never too early to start saving money. Set small, achievable goals like saving for your dream pair of sneakers, summer vacation, or even going to college.

Open a savings account at a bank and deposit a portion of your income each month. Not only will this help you develop the habit of saving, but it will also earn you some interest over time. Moreover, it's a good idea to save up an emergency fund so you're prepared when unexpected expenses arise, like a broken phone screen or a surprise birthday gift for your best friend.

Understand the Value of Credit

As a teen, you might not have your own credit card yet, but it is crucial to understand how credit works. Credit refers to the ability to borrow money with the promise to repay it later, often with interest.

Using credit wisely is essential for building a strong financial reputation and credit score, which will be important when you want to apply for a student loan or rent an apartment in the future. Start by learning good credit management habits from your parents or guardians, and only borrow what you know you can pay back on time.

Learn About Basic Investment and Financial Tools

Investing your money can help it grow, allowing you to achieve your financial goals faster. Familiarize yourself with investment basics like stocks and bonds and understand how they work. If you're unsure about investing, there are numerous online resources for beginners that can help you make informed choices.

Also, start exploring financial tools and apps that can help you with budgeting, tracking your expenses, and even investing. Developing these skills early on will set you up for long-term financial success.

Remember, the key to financial literacy is to be consistent, disciplined, and open to learning from your experiences. As your understanding of finances grows, you'll be better equipped to manage your money and make sound financial decisions throughout your life.

Common Misconceptions About Loans and Credit Cards and What You Can Do Instead

Many teenagers, even adults, have misconceptions about loans and credit cards, which can lead to bad money habits. Here are a few incorrect ideas you should be aware of, as well as what you can do instead:

Common Misconception #1: Loans and Credit Cards Are Expensive

You might think that taking out a loan or getting a credit card will automatically cost you an arm and a leg. However, this is not always the case—if used responsibly, loans and credit cards can actually help build up your credit score, which is essential for future financial success. Remember that when it comes to borrowing money or using credit cards, you get what you pay for—make sure you understand the terms of the agreement and read through any associated fees before signing on the dotted line.

Common Misconception #2: Taking Out Multiple Loans Will Help Your Credit Score

Some people may believe that multiple loans will help them have better financial standing in the long run. Unfortunately, this isn't true. In fact, having too much debt can negatively impact your credit score by showing potential lenders that you're unable to manage your finances responsibly. The best way to improve your credit score is by making regular payments on time and staying ahead of balances owed.

Common Misconception #3: You Should Only Get a Loan if You Absolutely Need It

An assumption around loans is that they should only take out a loan if they need it right away—however, this isn't necessarily true either. Taking out a loan when you don't absolutely need it can be beneficial because establishing a positive payment history with lenders helps build trust between parties over time and improves your overall creditworthiness. Before taking out a loan, make sure to assess how much you'll realistically be able to pay each month so as not to overextend yourself financially.

Overall, understanding how loans and credit cards work is vital so you know when (or when not) to use them responsibly. With proper knowledge about financial products like these, teens can set themselves up for long-term success with their finances!

Easy Ways to Manage Finances

In many cases, you can divide your income into four separate parts to help you track your habits: saving, spending, investing, and donating. Most purchases or desires will fall into one of these categories, and starting to separate your money from the beginning of your journey will help you get into the good habit of watching your income.

Saving Money

Saving money is crucial for financial stability. Begin by creating a budget and tracking your spending. Cut back on non-essential purchases, make an effort to stick to your budget, and try paying yourself first by putting some of your income into a savings account each month. Some tips to help you are:

- Set goals: Before you start saving, think about what you're saving for. Maybe it's a new pair of shoes, a concert ticket, or even college tuition—once you have a goal in mind, it becomes more exciting and easier to save.

- Open a savings account: Head to your local bank (with a parent or guardian) and open up a savings account. This will help you separate your spending money from the cash you're setting aside for your goals.

- Save a little each time: Each time you receive money (from your allowance, gifts, or a part-time job), try taking a portion of it (maybe 10% or 20%) and put it into your savings account. This will help you build your savings over time without feeling overwhelmed.

- Look for deals: Be a savvy shopper and look for sales, clearances, and deals when you do decide to spend money. Saving money on purchases will give you even more bang-for-your-buck!

Spending Money

Unfortunately, we work to then spend our hard-earned money. When spending your money, make sure you're mindful of what you're purchasing and how it fits into your budget. When considering a purchase, you must ask yourself some tough, soul-crushing questions like:

- Do I really need this?

- How will it benefit me?

- Is there an alternative that's cheaper?

- Could I save up for a better version of this in the future?

Answering these questions honestly can help you decide if your purchase is justified, and spending wisely now can help you save money in the long run. Here are a few tips to help you be strategic with your money.

- Create a budget: Start by writing down all income sources and list all monthly expenses, such as phone bills, food, entertainment, and any other recurring costs. Subtract the expenses from the income and determine how much money is left over; this is the amount that should be saved each month. This will help you see exactly where your money is going and how much you can afford to spend.

- Make smart choices: When it's time to spend your money, always think before you act. Ask yourself if you really need the item or if it can wait longer. This will help you avoid impulse purchases and keep you on track financially.

- Use cash or debit cards: Avoid using credit cards as they can lead to overspending and debt.

Instead, use cash or a debit card to help you stay within your budget.

Investing Money

Investing can be a little confusing, but it's a great way to grow your money over time. When you invest, you purchase an asset that may appreciate in value and generate income (e.g., stocks, bonds). Investing can be intimidating for beginners, and we'll review this more in the following sections, but here are some tips to get started:

- Learn the basics: Spend time learning about the stock market and different types of investments like mutual funds, bonds, and stocks. There are tons of resources online to help you understand the basics.

- Start small: As a teen, you'll likely only have a small amount of money to invest. That's perfectly fine—start with what you have and build your investment over time.

- Get help: Seek advice from trusted adults like parents, teachers, or family friends who have knowledge and experience in investing. They'll be able to guide you through your first investments and answer any questions you might have.

Even the smallest investment, like putting away $30 a month, can add up over time. By investing wisely, you'll be able to grow your money and achieve financial independence in no time!

Investment Calculator

Starting early gives you a significant advantage over others who begin investing later in life. This is due to the magic of compounding interest, which means your investments will grow faster over time. So, let's dive into how an investment calculator works.

Begin With the Basics: Open a Checking and Savings Account

Before you start investing, you'll need a place to save your money. Opening a checking and savings account is a perfect first step. Since you're under 18, you might need to open a joint account with your parents at their financial institution. This account will help you keep your spending money (checking) separate from your savings, which will be used for investing.

Explore Investment Options

Now that you've got a place to save your money, it's time to learn about different investing options. You can talk to an investment specialist, like a financial advisor, for guidance. One option you could explore is a "Roth 401k for juniors"—a retirement savings plan designed specifically for young investors like you. This type of account allows your investments to grow tax-free, which means you'll have even more money to enjoy when you retire.

Diversify Your Investment Portfolio

To invest effectively, spread your money across different investments. This is called diversification, and it helps reduce the risk of losing all your money if one investment doesn't perform well. Start small and divide your investments among different portfolios, such as savings accounts, stocks, and retirement plans like a 401k.

Be Consistent With Your Contributions

One key to successful investing is consistently putting money into your investments. Even if you can only contribute 10 percent of your allowance, make it a habit to do so each time you receive it. This consistent saving will add up over time, and thanks to compounding interest, your money will grow even faster. No matter what, try to avoid skipping contributions—every bit counts!

Overall, an investment calculator can help you understand how your investments will grow over time, depending on factors such as the amount you invest, the types of investments you choose, and the consistency of your contributions. By starting early, diversifying your portfolio, and staying consistent, you can build a solid financial foundation for your future.

Donating Money

You certainly don't have to donate your money. There are other ways you can give back to your community, like volunteering your time or participating in charity events. But if you choose to donate money, make sure your money is going toward a cause you believe in. Here are a few tips:

- Choose a cause: Find something that you feel passionately about, whether it's animal welfare, environmental issues, or giving back to your community. Supporting a cause close to your heart will make donating feel even more rewarding.

- Research different organizations: Before making a donation, do some research on the organizations that support your chosen cause. Look for non-profits with an excellent reputation and a clear mission.

- Volunteer your time: If you don't have much money to donate, consider volunteering your time instead. This makes a difference and is a valuable learning experience for you as well.

So, there you have it! By following these easy steps, you'll be well on your way to becoming a teen finance pro.

Good Finance and Spending Habits

Good finance and spending habits are key to success later in life. Here are a few tips to help teens get started:

- Track spending: Download an app or keep a paper ledger of receipts to track how much you spend each day. This will help teens become more aware of where their money is going and give them a better sense of control over their finances.

- Set financial goals: Having specific financial goals can help teens stay motivated to build good habits in money management. Goals can include saving for college tuition, or a new car or working toward being able to afford something they've wanted for a while.

- Automate savings: Setting up automatic transfers into savings accounts can help keep teens on track with their budgeting goals by taking out the guesswork of having to manually transfer funds every month.

- Stay informed: Staying informed about current news topics related to personal finances, such as investing and retirement planning, can help teens have better conversations with their parents or trusted advisors about managing money effectively in the long term.

Teen Appropriate Ways to Make Money

Sadly, our wants, needs, and experiences all cost money. It's hard for teenagers to find ways to make some extra cash, especially when faced with age restrictions by employers. Here are some ways you can make some money without having to get a traditional job:

- Babysitting: This classic money-making opportunity is perfect for you if you're responsible and love being around kids. Get started by asking your neighbors, family, and friends, or use an app to find babysitting jobs. Pro tip: Take a babysitting and first-aid course to become a certified babysitter, making you even more in demand, and don't forget to always consult with your parents or guardians before taking on any jobs!

- Dog walking or pet sitting: Are you an animal lover? Turn that passion into a job by offering to walk dogs or pet sit for neighbors and friends. You can also create a profile on Rover.com and extend your services to a wider community. Be reliable and maintain good communication with the pet parents, and you'll soon have a list of happy clients!

- Sell homemade goods: Are you creative and talented in making handmade stuff like jewelry, art, or baked goods? Sell your creations at local craft fairs, farmer's markets, or even online on Etsy. Make sure to factor in the cost of materials, and always take pride in producing high-quality products.

- Tutoring: Is there a subject you excel in? Offer your services as a tutor, either in-person or online. Reach out to classmates, family, and friends, or post on social media. You can also join websites like Tutor.com or Wyzant.com to connect with potential clients. Be prepared with helpful resources and show patience and understanding with your students.

- Yard work: Help out your neighbors with yard work such as mowing lawns, raking leaves, or shoveling snow. This teaches you the value of hard work, and it's an excellent way to stay active. Plus, you can make a lasting positive impression by transforming someone's messy yard into a beautiful oasis.

- Social media management: Are you always on top of the latest social media trends? Offer your services to local businesses or even to your parents, helping them manage their social media accounts. This can be a beneficial way to learn about marketing and entrepreneurship and enhance your tech skills.

- Start a YouTube channel or a blog: Many teens are now becoming successful YouTubers or bloggers, showcasing their talents, or sharing their thoughts on various topics. Keep in mind this option might take longer to earn money, but it's an amazing way to pursue your passion and gain valuable experience in content creation and marketing. Always make sure to produce quality work, meaning the healthy materials, that can help others, in order to contribute to a higher standard within your network.

Don't forget that no matter which job you choose, always be determined, reliable, and professional. Not only will you earn money, but you'll also develop valuable skills that will last a lifetime. Now, go on and explore these teen-friendly money-making ideas and start earning cash today.

Remember, the most important thing is just to get started. The sooner you begin investing, the more time your money has to grow. So, take that first step and open a savings account, start exploring investment options, and watch your money begin to work for you.

Reflection Questions

Do you have any expenses? What do you normally pay for?

_____

_____

_____

_____

_____

_____

_____

_____

Do you have a part-time job? If so, what do you do, and how much do you make?

_____

_____

_____

_____

_____

_____

_____

_____

What jobs would you be interested in trying?

_____

_____

_____

_____

_____

_____

_____

How do you plan to save money and invest wisely? If so, how?

_____

_____

_____

_____

_____

259

Do you have a bank account? If so, what type of account is it, and how do you use it?

What are some future saving goals that you would like to achieve?

_____

_____

_____

_____

What is your current experience with money? How would you like to change or improve your experience with money?

_____

_____

_____

_____

_____

_____

_____

_____

Chapter 16:

Goals and Focuses

Bradley and Bernadette were as close as siblings despite not being biologically related. They were the kind of friends who had shared interests and had been supporting each other's individual pursuits.

Bradley was passionate about music, always practicing his guitar to perfect his skills to achieve his goal of becoming a professional guitar player. Bernadette, on the other hand, was very curious about space and the universe, so her focus was more on studying astronomy and learning everything she could about the cosmos.

One evening, as they were hanging out at their favorite spot under an old, big tree, they started talking about their dreams and futures. Bradley, being goal-oriented, explained his clear and specific aspiration to Bernadette: he wanted to be the solo guitar player in a famous band someday.

Bernadette, puzzled by Bradley's goal, asked, "What's the difference between having a goal like yours and me focusing on learning about astronomy?"

Bradley thought for a moment and replied, "A goal is like a target we aim for, a specific outcome that we want to achieve. For me, it's becoming a musician. It's something I can work toward, measure my progress, and eventually reach. So, I try to put most of my focus on this goal."

As Bradley kicked around an apple on the ground, he continued, "Having a goal gives me direction and motivation to stay focused. Knowing that I have a deadline, like school recitals and different show tryouts, helps me push myself to work harder and get traction to beat the competition in getting that coveted spot."

Bernadette nodded, understanding his point of view but still curious about where her focus on astronomy fell in comparison. She asked, "So where does my focus on space and the universe fit into this picture?"

Bradley smiled and said, "A focus, unlike a goal, is more about dedicating yourself to learning, exploring, and engaging deeply in a specific area of interest. In your case, it's astronomy. By focusing on it, you don't necessarily have a specific endpoint or a particular achievement in mind, but rather, you're continually expanding your knowledge, skills, and passion in that subject."

"Think of it this way," Bradley continued, "When I set a goal, I might hit that target, feel satisfied, and be done with it. But when you have a focus, it's like you never stop growing and exploring because there's always more to learn and discover."

Bernadette's eyes lit up, realizing that her focus on astronomy didn't have to be measured by a specific achievement, but instead, it was a never-ending journey of discovery and deepening her understanding of the universe. Both goal setting and having areas of focus were important in helping them navigate their lives and grow as individuals.

As you can see, a goal is the aim or desired result, and it's the best to be time boxed. It is something that you work toward and strive to achieve over time. A focus, on the other hand, is what helps you stay on track and stay motivated in achieving your goals. Focus is the ability to concentrate on something while tuning out distractions or sidetracks. Having both a goal and focus allows you to stay organized, have a plan of action, and take small steps every day that lead to achieving your end result. Focusing helps teens prioritize their tasks and activities in order to reach their goals efficiently and effectively.

Why Is Goal Setting Important?

Goal setting is super important for teens like you, and it's not just about getting good grades or acing tests. It's about shaping your entire life and aligning yourself with who you truly are. So why exactly is goal setting a big deal? Let me break this down for you.

- Builds confidence: When you set goals, you're creating a plan to achieve them. Each time you hit a milestone or achieve your goal, it gives you a rush of confidence and self-belief that you can do anything you set your mind to. Plus, having a clear vision of your future helps you feel more secure and grounded as you navigate the rollercoaster ride that is teenage life.

- Improves focus: As a teenager, you've got a million things going on—school, sports, hobbies, friends, and social media. Goal setting helps you stay focused and prioritize what's truly important to you. It acts as a roadmap, guiding you to your desired destination and helping you avoid getting distracted by unnecessary detours.

- Teaches responsibility: When you set goals, you're essentially taking control of your life and making a promise to yourself to work toward them. This teaches you to be responsible and accountable for your actions, which are essential skills you'll need as you grow into adulthood.

- Develop good habits: To achieve your goals, you'll have to put in the work and develop good habits, like organizing your time, managing your finances, and staying disciplined. These habits are crucial in your journey toward personal growth and will benefit you throughout your life.

- Enhances decision-making skills: Working toward your goals requires you to make tough decisions at times. By setting goals and working systematically toward them, you'll get better at navigating those hard choices and making decisions that align with your values and priorities.

- Encourages growth and self-improvement: Through goal setting, you're constantly assessing your strengths, weaknesses, and progress toward your goals. This helps you understand your areas for improvement, prompting you to keep learning and developing your skills.

- Provides motivation and a sense of purpose: Having goals gives you something to strive for. They act as a driving force, motivating you to push through challenges and overcome obstacles. Plus, working toward goals makes you feel like you have a rational purpose in life, giving you a greater sense of fulfillment and happiness overall.

- Sets you up for success in the future: You see, by setting goals now and working toward them as a teen, you're actually ahead of the game. Not only are you learning valuable life skills, but you're also setting yourself up for success in your adult life—whether that's in your career, relationships, or personal achievements.

So, there you have it! Goal setting is cool, important, and super beneficial for teens like you. It's not just about scoring A's or winning at sports—it's about preparing for all the amazing things life has in store for you.

How to Set SMART Goals?

Goal setting is an essential skill that will help you accomplish your dreams quickly and efficiently. One technique to master this skill is by setting SMART goals. Don't worry—it's not as complicated as it sounds. By the end of this, you'll know how to set goals that are specific, measurable, attainable, relevant, and time bound (Yourtherapysource, 2022).

So, let's break down each criterion of a SMART goal, and see how you can use them in your life.

Specific

When you set a goal, it's crucial to be specific about what you want. A vague goal like "I want to be healthier" or "I want to do well in school" isn't going to cut it. A specific goal will give you a clear path to stay focused. To make your goal more specific, ask yourself::

- What exactly do I want to achieve?

- Why is this goal important to me?

- How can I accomplish this goal?

For example, instead of saying, "I want to be healthier," a specific goal could be "I want to eat five servings of fruits and vegetables daily and exercise for 30 minutes at least four times a week."

Measurable

Now that you have a specific goal, it's time to make it measurable. This means attaching a number or a concrete result to your goal to track your progress. To make your goal measurable, ask yourself:

- How much or how many?

- How will I know when I've reached my goal?

For instance, the specific goal mentioned above—eating a specific number of servings of fruits and vegetables— can be easily tracked, and you'll know that you've reached your goal when you're consistently achieving that.

Attainable

It's essential to be realistic when setting goals. While it's good to dream big, setting unattainable goals can lead to disappointment and negatively impact your motivation. So, ensure that your goal is achievable given your current resources, time, and skill set. To check if your goal is attainable, consider the following:

- Is this goal realistic given my current situation?

- Am I able to commit the time and effort to reach this goal?

For example, if you have limited access to a gym or fitness equipment, you might need to adjust your goal to include more accessible kinds of exercise.

Relevant

Your goals should be aligned with your values and broader interests in life. Setting relevant goals ensures that you're working toward something that truly matters to you. Evaluate your goal by asking:

- Does this goal align with my values and long-term objectives?

- Is this goal beneficial to my growth and development?

For instance, focusing on personal health and wellness is relevant to your overall well-being and happiness.

Time-Bound

Finally, your goal needs a clear timeframe. Setting a deadline keeps you accountable and helps you monitor your progress. To make your goal time-bound, establish a target date or a specific period for completion. Ask yourself:

- When do I want to achieve this goal?

- What can I accomplish within the next few weeks or months?

For example, you might set a goal to establish a healthier routine within the next three months. Then you assemble it to create your SMART goal.

And there you have it—that's how you set SMART goals! This approach will make sure your goals are clear, achievable, and relevant, ultimately helping you pave the way to a successful adulthood. So go ahead and give it a try—your dreams are waiting!

Now that you know what SMART goals are and how they work, use the matrix below to break down some of your current goals. The first one is done for you as an example.

	SMART Goal	Criteria	Description
1	*Raising my grade by 7 points, from 76 to 83, in 4 weeks, so that I can improve my education and harness my self-control.*	Specific	*I want to increase my grades because good grades guaranties getting accepted to college*
		Measurable	*Currently, I am a C student. I want to raise my grade to a B in a month.*
		Attainable	*This goal is very attainable. I have 12 weeks left of school, and my last grade was a high C (76). I need four weeks to bring my grade up 7 points. (83) at least.*
		Relevant	*This goal is relevant to my education and long-term effects in adulthood. If I can harness my self-control now, and improve my grades through hard work and effort, then I will improve the tools I need to accomplish other challenges in adulthood.*

		Time-Bound	*My goal is to accomplish this in 4 weeks. With 12 weeks left of school, I have enough time to reevaluate my goals and change or adjust as needed.*
2			

3			

How to Stay Focused on Your Goals?

You can start to stay focused on your goals by following a few simple steps.

- Set goals: The first step to staying focused is setting attainable and realistic goals. Identifying what you want to achieve provides clarity and direction, which can help motivate you to stay on track. Set specific goals that are measurable so progress can be monitored.

- Make a plan: Once you've identified your goals, create a plan to reach them. Break down each goal into smaller, more manageable tasks, and make sure to take the necessary steps each day or week to reach them. Having an action plan helps prevent procrastination and keeps you from getting off-track with your goals.

- Prioritize: Establishing priorities is essential for keeping yourself focused on achieving your goals. Prioritizing tasks allows for better time management when tackling projects or assignments, as well as prevents distractions from taking over your attention. Decide which tasks need your immediate attention, then work toward completing those before moving on to the next task in line.

- Eliminate distractions: Avoiding distractions or procrastination will help keep you moving forward with reaching your goals while having the added benefit of improving concentration levels when doing work or studying for exams. Try reducing time on social media sites, turning off phone notifications, or just putting away any digital devices when attempting any type of task that requires focus and concentration.

- Celebrate your successes: Finally, celebrating successes is critical for motivation and keeping yourself energized when working toward reaching a goal! Achieving milestones along the way is an excellent way of staying motivated throughout the process while also reinforcing positive behavior that leads to success!

Identify Steps to Achieve Your Goals

When you have a specific goal, breaking them down into more manageable pieces will help you stay focused without feeling overwhelmed or falling behind. Using the SMART goals you created in the previous Matrix, break them down into the smallest steps to make them easier for you to tackle. Break the task into as many steps as you need (use the following rows if you need more room), and also add any resources or people you can use to help you complete the goal. Continuing with the good grades example, the first is done for your guidance.

	SMART Goal	**Step 1**	**Step 2**	**Step 3**
1	*My goal is to raise my grade by 7 points, from a 76 to an 83, in 4 weeks so that I can improve my education and harness my self-control.*	*Evaluate my current standing to determine my strengths and weaknesses.*	*Make a list of my weaknesses and find the content or resources I need to review.*	*Include 30 to 60 minute study sessions into my daily routine.*
2				
3				

Time Box Your Visions

An amazing way to keep track of your goals and progress is to have a timeline or checklist that you can refer to through. Below are several matrices to help you break down your large goals into smaller micro goals. To begin, take one of your SMART goals that you created in the other matrix in this chapter, the step breakdowns you made in the second matrix, and follow the prompts to create more manageable goals. Using weight loss and fitness goals as an example, the first row is completed for you to show how to tackle your situation.

3 Months Checklist				
	SMART Goal	3 Month Goal	Steps to Get There	Result?
1	*Lose twenty pounds in a year*	*—Lose five pounds* *—Workout three times a week*	*—Drink more water* *—Eat healthier meals*	✓
2				
3				

		6 Months Checklist		
	SMART Goal	**6 Month Goal**	**Steps to get there**	**Result?**
1	*Lose twenty pounds in a year*	*—Lose another five pounds (10 total)* *—Workout four times a week*	*—Drink more water* *—Add a strength training or resistance day* *—Eat more healthy foods* *—Follow a regular sleep schedule*	✓
2				
3				

9 Months Checklist

	SMAR T Goal	9 Month Goal	Steps needed to get there	Result?
1	Lose twenty pounds in a year	−Down 10 pounds, now it's time to lose another five −Workout five times a week	−Join a workout program with others −Start a meal plan −Follow a regular sleep schedule	✔
2				
3				

12 Months Checklist				
	SMART Goal	**12 Month Goal**	**Steps to get there**	**Result?**
1	*Lose twenty pounds in a year*	*–Down 15 pounds, now it's time to lose the last five* *–Workout six times a week, include an "active rest" day*	*–Improve my meal plan* *–Revisit my sleep schedule* *–Walk 2 miles a day*	✓
2				
3				

SMART Goal Matrix Sample

This matrix is the summary of all the previous tables to help you understand how all that information can simply fit in one place. The first and most relevant example is done for you, so using what you have learnt from this chapter, and this matrix, you can easily continue to document your own to set your SMART goals moving forward over, and over!

	SMART Goal	Criteria	Description	Steps	Result Duration
1	Raising my grade by 7 points, from 76 to 83, in 4 weeks, so that I can improve my education and harness my self-control.	Specific	I want to increase my grades because good grades guaranties getting accepted to college	Evaluate my current standing to determine my strengths and weaknesses.	30% 1st Month
		Measurable	Currently, I am a C student. I want to raise my grade to a B in a month.	Make a list of my weaknesses and find the content or resources I need to review	
		Attainable	This goal is very attainable. I have 12 weeks left of school, and my last grade was a high C (76). I need four weeks to bring my grade up 7 points. (83) at least.	Include 30 to 60 minute study sessions into my	

| | | Relevant | This goal is relevant to my education and long-term effects in adulthood. If I can harness my self-control now, and improve my grades through hard work and effort, then I will improve the tools I need to accomplish other challenges in adulthood. | daily routine.

Give myself weekly assessments and document progress notes.

Identify areas I need help with and try them one by one. I can ask | |

		Time-Bound	My goal is to accomplish this in one month (4 weeks). With 12 weeks left of school, I have more than enough time to reevaluate my goals and change or adjust as needed.	the school for more textbooks or materials. I can also ask for a tutor in the after-school program. I can tell my parents I'm struggling with my plan and ask if they can help me with unfamiliar material.	
2					

Daily Checklists

Begin creating your routine and list your chores or responsibilities. Use the guides to help you organize your daily tasks and cross those you met off your list.

286

Daily To-Do List

Task	Completed?
Walk and feed the dogs	✓

Mind Maps for Blocked Ideas

Blocked ideas can make an outcome feel impossible to reach. However, sometimes a good brainstorming session is all you need to determine your next path. Below are two mind maps to help you with any stuck ideas you may have. It doesn't matter where you are stuck or how deep you are into your goal; you can always make a mind map to help you see all the routes you can take so you can decide which is best for you.

In the center goes your main idea, whether it's a smart goal like improving your grades or just a plan to make more money and improve your life. Then you use the branches to create sub-ideas or goals that relate to your first one.

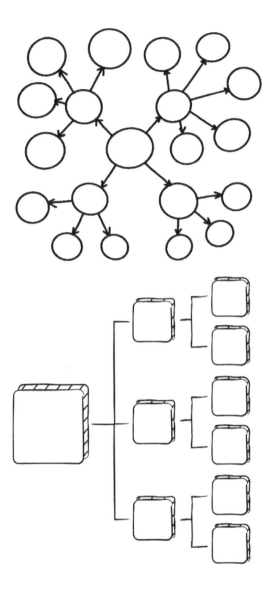

Celebration Ideas

Probably the best parts of working toward your goals are the celebrations and rewards. Use the space below to brainstorm all the different ways you would like to celebrate or reward yourself for every milestone. For every reward, give yourself a check mark (even if you do it multiple times), and after you finish your goal, count how many rewards you racked up!

Reward or Celebration	Result?

Don't forget to periodically pat yourself on the back for achieving a few steps and look forward to the remainder of the steps to be able to celebrate a milestone, even if it is small. Include those who helped you in your accomplishments and thank them for helping to improve your achievements even further.

Reflection Questions

Do you set goals often? Which types of goals do you set?

_____

_____

_____

_____

_____

_____

_____

Have you used the SMART method before? If so, did it help you?

_____

_____

_____

_____

_____

_____

What strategies do you use to keep yourself on track with your goals?

Do you find it easy or difficult to stay focused on your goals? Why?

_____

_____

_____

Where do you struggle with goal setting? What can you do to improve this?

_____

_____

_____

_____

_____

_____

_____

How do you reward yourself for achieving or making progress toward a goal?

_____

_____

_____

_____

Do you believe that celebrating successes is important for motivation? Why or why not?

Chapter 17:

Maps, Directions, and

Instructions

Bradley and Bernadette both share a passion for hiking and exploring the great outdoors. One day, they decided to go on a hike to a nearby mountain. Bradley knew the trail well, but Bernadette had never been there before.

Bradley pulled out a map to show Bernadette the route they would take. He explained that the map had symbols that represented different elements, such as mountains, rivers, and trails. Bradley taught Bernadette how to read the map key and legend, which helped her understand the symbols better.

He also explained the scale on the map that she could use to measure the distance between two points on the map. This was important so they wouldn't get lost along the way.

After a brief lesson, Bradley turned to Bernadette and asked if she understood how to read the map. She nodded, confident enough to help. Soon they began their trek up the mountain.

It was an arduous hike, but they finally made it to the top. As they made their way back, Bernadette wanted to take a different trail. She knew it wasn't on the map, so she asked Bradley to give her directions. Bradley gave her clear and concise directions using north, south, east, and west. Bernadette used the sun and her watch to know which direction was which.

Bradley reminded her to pay attention to symbols along the way, such as trees and rocks to help her remember the right path. In a matter of no time, they reached their destination.

From this experience, Bernadette learned how to read a map and take and give directions. Bradley's patient and informative teaching allowed her to gain the necessary skills to navigate through different environments. She realized how important it was to be prepared and knowledgeable when exploring new places, which made her more confident and excited to take on new adventures.

With the new technology, almost everyone has access to a smartphone, and different apps, which makes it easy to navigate around. However, it's still useful to learn how to read a paper map and navigate your way out in case it's needed, or let's say if your phone is dead!

It's also helpful to know how to ask or give directions to someone else.

Basics of Directions and Reading a Map

Understanding directions and maps is an essential skill that can come in handy in various situations, such as hiking, traveling, or finding your way in new and unfamiliar places. So, let's break it down to the basics and make it easy for you to understand.

Firstly, let's take a look at the compass rose. It is the circular diagram found on most maps and represents the four cardinal directions of north, south, east, and west. These are usually represented by the initials N, S, E, and W, respectively.

Then there are the four intercardinal directions, which are northeast (NE), northwest (NW), southeast (SE), and southwest (SW). Now that we know the cardinal and intercardinal directions, let's talk about reading maps. Maps typically contain symbols for physical features such as rivers, roads, and mountains. Additionally, they have a scale to measure distances from one point to another.

To locate an exact point on the map, you need to understand the coordinates, which is a combination of the latitude and longitude lines. Latitude lines are the horizontal lines on the map, while longitude lines are the vertical lines. The point where these lines intersect is your location's coordinate.

To find your way, you need to understand how to read the legend. The map legend is usually a small table, or a box located at the bottom of the map, which explains the symbols and colors used on the map.

A few more terms to know are the scale, which indicates distance measurement on the map, and the contour lines, which show the elevation levels of the map area.

So how does one read a map? Here's a step-by-step guide:

- Locate your current position on the map using the compass rose and coordinates

- Identify the location you want to navigate to

- Determine the scale to understand the distance between both points

- Plan your route using the map legend and symbols

- Use the contour lines on the map to understand elevation changes between locations

Giving Directions

Giving directions is an important skill that everyone should learn. It can help you communicate with others and guide them to their desired location. As a teenager, you may need to give directions to your friends or family members who are new to the area. Here are some tips to help you give directions:

- Use clear and concise language: When giving directions, use simple and easy-to-understand words. Avoid using complicated vocabulary or technical terms that might confuse the person you are directing. For example, say, "Turn left" instead of "Take a left-hand turn." It's also helpful to give one or two directions at a time so the other person isn't overwhelmed but also has enough information to know what to do.

- Start with a landmark: Landmarks are easy-to-identify objects that can help the person navigate their way. For example, you could say, "Start at the big red brick building on Main Street."

- Use street names: Street names are important when giving directions. Make sure to include the name of the street the person should turn onto or walk along. For instance, you can say, "Turn right onto Elm Street."

- Give distances: It can be helpful to give the person you're directing a sense of how far they need to go. "It's about three blocks down on the left-hand side" is a simple way to clarify your directions.

- Use visual cues: Visual cues are another great way to help someone navigate. For instance, you could say, "Take the second left after the blue mailbox."

- Be patient: Remember that some people may not be familiar with the area and may need extra guidance. Be patient and willing to repeat directions if necessary.

Taking Directions

As a teenager, you need to learn how to take and listen to directions. Sometimes, you may find yourself in unfamiliar places where you need guidance to reach your destination. Following instructions from others is essential not only for your success but also for your safety.

Here are tips to help you with directional skills:

- Stay Calm and Focused: When someone is giving you directions, make sure you stay calm and focused. Avoid distraction and pay attention to what the person is saying. Make eye contact to show you are interested in what they are saying.

- Ask for Clarification: If you do not understand something, do not hesitate to ask for clarification. The person giving the direction is there to help you; therefore, it is okay to ask for more information. Repeat the directions back to them to verify you understood them correctly.

- Confirm the Destination: Before you start your journey, verify the destination with the person giving the directions. Ensure you understand the directions and the place you intend to go to. This way, you will prevent getting lost along the way.

- Politely Decline if Necessary: If you do not trust the person giving you directions, politely decline and seek directions from someone else. Remember that your safety is a top priority, and you should never put yourself in harm's way.

- Express Gratitude: Once you have received the directions, express gratitude by saying thank you. It is polite and shows appreciation to the person who offered to help you. Always maintain a friendly tone throughout the conversation.

The Basics to Instructions

There are instances that you'll need to read an instruction, either on a desk that you just bought in a box and needs to be assembled, or how to use a blender, or even how to do certain tests or junior job interviews.

As a teenager, it can be overwhelming to follow directions and instructions, especially if they involve complex tasks or situations. However, there are some helpful tips and tricks that can make the process easier and more manageable.

First, approach every set of instructions with a positive attitude and an open mind. It's easy to get frustrated or discouraged if you don't understand something right away, but taking a deep breath and reminding yourself that you can do it can make a big difference.

Next, it's crucial to read the instructions carefully and thoroughly, from start to finish. Don't skip over any steps or assume that you know what to do without reading the directions first. If you're dealing with written instructions, try highlighting or underlining key points to help you remember them.

As you're going through the instructions, take the time to fully understand each step before moving on to the next one. It's like building a puzzle—you can't put the pieces together if you don't have a clear idea of what each one looks like first. Read the booklet or directions all the way through one time without completing anything to see what the overall project, design, or route looks like.

This will help you break down and understand the task at hand. If you're still confused by a particular step, don't be afraid to ask for help or clarification.

Another helpful tip is to break down complex instructions into smaller, more manageable tasks. For example, if you're putting together a piece of furniture, focus on assembling one section at a time rather than trying to tackle the entire thing in one go.

Finally, if you need to give instructions to someone else, take the time to confirm that they understand each step. This can be especially important in situations like medical procedures or job interviews, where there's little room for error.

By following these tips and approaching each set of instructions with patience and confidence, you can successfully navigate even the most challenging situations with ease.

Reflection Questions

Have you had to give directions in the past? If so, what did you do? Was the experience a success?

_____

_____

_____

_____

_____

_____

_____

How confident do you feel giving someone directions? What tricks and tips might you already have?

_____

_____

_____

_____

_____

How do you navigate a situation if the instructions you're reading seem too complicated?

What strategies do you use to remember important information when following directions or instructions?

What might you be able to do if you think you are lost or are misunderstanding some directions? What is the best way to express gratitude after someone has given you directions?

In what situations might it be important to confirm that someone else understands your directions? What are the consequences of not doing this?

Chapter 18:

Safe Commute and Learning

to Drive

Getting to places safely is crucial for everyone, especially teenagers who are often trying to navigate new places and environments on their own. Suppose you've been walking yourself to school, the public library, nearby shops, parks, etc. In that case, you're already aware of the responsibility that comes with being out there alone without adult supervision. Whether you're walking, biking, or skateboarding, taking steps to minimize risks and protect yourself on the road is crucial.

For starters, understanding and obeying traffic rules is essential. This means knowing and following traffic signals, staying in designated lanes, and using crosswalks when available. Even if you're in a hurry, rushing or cutting corners can lead to accidents, so it's always better to slow down and stay aware of your surroundings. Furthermore, using proper safety gear like helmets, knee guards, and reflective clothing can help reduce the chance of injury in case of an accident.

It's also important to be conscious of your surroundings and pay attention to what's going on around you. Whether you're walking alone or with friends, it's easy to get distracted by your phone, music, or conversations, but keeping your senses attuned to your environment could save your life. Avoid walking through dark, deserted areas and stay on well-lit paths and roads. Make sure you know the safest route to your destination and stick to it, especially if you're in an unfamiliar area. Make sure listening to music on your headset or earbuds isn't preventing you from hearing what's happening around you!

Additionally, it's always useful to have emergency contacts saved in your phone or written down somewhere you can easily access them. Also, keep yourself informed about the latest road rules and the best ways to stay safe while traveling. Stay up-to-date on updates, follow your driving school's lessons and instructions, if applicable to you, and talk to your peers, so you can stay safe, healthy, and ready to explore the world safely.

Older Teens and Driving

For older teens, learning to drive is a significant and exciting milestone. It's also very useful as you'll be able to drive yourself or your siblings to school or to nearby shopping centers without having to ask your parents or others. It can offer you tremendous benefits such as independence, time management, and convenience. However, to achieve these benefits, it's vital that you approach driving education with the seriousness it deserves and recognize its significant impact on the driver and society at large. As driving is not just about getting from point A to point B. It is also about the safety of everyone in the car and on the road.

Most importantly, understanding the rules of the road is vital for driving success. This knowledge includes traffic signals, road signs, speed limits, and basic driving laws. It's recommended to study these rules from a reliable source, such as a driver's education textbook or online resources. Additionally, consider the risks associated with driving and how to minimize them. These risks include distracted driving, impaired driving, and aggressive driving, among others.

Acquiring practical skills is equally crucial when preparing for driving. The best way to achieve this is by seeking out a professional driving instructor or a veteran driver to teach you. A professional instructor's role is to teach you not only the techniques of driving but also the nuances of vehicle maneuvering, anticipation, and collision avoidance. They also help you identify your strengths and weaknesses and work on them accordingly. A veteran driver, on the other hand, can provide valuable insights and tips based on their real-life experience.

Moreover, it's imperative to practice consistently to master the necessary skills. Practicing in different types of weather and road conditions, with your instructor, can increase your confidence and comfort level while driving by yourself later. Taking advantage of the permitted hours of supervised driving in your region is an excellent way to gain hands-on experience with a trusted companion.

Let me tell you a story about Bernadette and Bradley's learning to drive and it has impacted their lives.

16-year-old Bernadette had always been nervous about driving for a very unknown reason. That's why, she wasn't excited to be behind the wheel of a car, until the time came that she had to start taking driving lessons. Bradley, on the other hand, had been dreaming about getting his driver's license for the last four years, since he was 12. He had studied the driving manual cover to cover and had practiced driving with his dad since he was old enough to reach the pedals.

One day, Bradley offered to give Bernadette a ride to a movie. Bernadette was hesitant at first but decided to take him up on his offer. As they drove down the highway, Bernadette started to feel more and more nervous. She kept checking her phone and fidgeting with the radio. Bradley noticed her unease and asked her what was wrong.

Bernadette admitted that she feared driving. She then mentioned watching other teens driving, reminds her of her fear, as she didn't feel prepared for the responsibility of being behind the wheel. Bradley assured her that he had felt the same way before he started driving and that with practice and patience, she would gain confidence and become a competent driver.

After that conversation, Bernadette started taking driving lessons seriously. She signed up for a driving school behind the wheel program, listened carefully to her instructor's advice, and practiced driving with her parents every weekend. Within a few months, she had not only passed her driving test but was also comfortable driving at night or with her friend Bradley.

A few months later, when the summer break started, Bradley and Bernadette planned to go on a half a day road trip. They packed their bags and set off in Bernadette's dad's car. Along the way, Bradley noticed Bernadette's proper driving, obeying the speed limit, and maintaining a safe distance from other cars. He was impressed by her driving skills, which was the direct result of proper training and practice.

Pros and Cons of Driving

With teen driving, there are both pros and cons. On one hand, driving can provide freedom and independence, allowing you to go wherever you please. However, it can also lead to dangerous situations if not handled responsibly.

To prepare for the concerns of teen driving, there are several things you can do Firstly, make sure to get trained by a professional. Many insurance companies also offer discounts to new drivers who have completed a professional driving course, to encourage new drivers to get trained properly. This will give you the necessary skills to handle different situations on the road from the beginning before you start building bad habits, which is more difficult to correct later.

Practicing in an empty parking lot before testing your skills on the actual road can be very helpful. This will give you a chance to learn each major technique and become more comfortable driving. Don't be afraid to use a student or new driver sign, on your car to let others know. It may help you avoid dangerous situations.

Another tip to keep in mind is that highway driving can be more dangerous than local roads. On the highway, we travel at higher speeds, which means we have less time to react. Be sure to stay aware of your surroundings and pay extra attention when driving on highways, especially during rush hour traffic. Pay close attention to other drivers, and always look ahead for potential risks. However, If you're just starting out, it might be helpful to stick to the streets for the first year or so until you become more comfortable driving.

Furthermore, it's great to have a parent or experienced driver sitting beside you to advise and correct you if needed, even after obtaining your driver's license. Taking it slow, driving in daylight and non-rush hours, as well as not having unnecessary passengers can all help you build up your confidence and stay safe on the road.

Also, make sure that you talk to them about their insurance policies and any roadside assistance policies they may have, that you're a listed driver, and that you understand how to use them in an emergency.

While there are pros and cons to teen driving, remember that driving is a big responsibility. By taking the necessary precautions and driving responsibly, you can enjoy the benefits that driving provides while staying safe on the road. So, remember, always drive with caution, and be prepared for any situation that may arise.

Reflection Questions

Do you drive already? If not, are you planning to? What are some concerns or excitements you may have?

_____

_____

_____

_____

_____

_____

_____

What are some pros and cons that come with the responsibility of driving?

_____

_____

_____

_____

_____

_____

_____

_____

If you do drive, do you think you're a good driver? What are some of your strengths and weaknesses when it comes to driving?

_____

_____

_____

_____

_____

_____

_____

What are some ways you would like to try practicing your driving skills?

_____

_____

_____

_____

If you've already been practicing, what are some techniques that have worked for you? What didn't work?

Chapter 19:

Planning for Your Future

On a weekend afternoon, they decided to meet up at their favorite park to discuss their newly formed dreams and aspirations. Now Bradley realized professional guitar player wasn't his ideal career and was excited about his future as an engineer, while Bernadette also switched her focus and dreamed of becoming a successful entrepreneur. "But how do we get there?" Bradley questioned as they sat under the shade of their favorite tree.

Then, Bernadette remembered her teacher's advice on future planning for teenagers. "Well," she started, "future planning is all about thinking ahead and making decisions to help us succeed. When we plan, we take proactive steps to secure our future success."

Bradley looked intrigued, "By proactive steps, you mean we need to figure out the necessary actions to turn our dreams into reality?"

"Exactly!" Bernadette responded. She then pulled out her notepad, and they began writing down their ambitions, ways to achieve them, and the timeline.

The first proactive step they decided to take was to research their chosen fields in depth. They began visiting libraries, browsing the Internet, emailing experts, and attending workshops. Then they took courses that strengthened their skills and used their free time to read books and engage in relevant activities.

Another vital step was to build a strong network of connections with another like-minded groups and individuals. They joined clubs and organizations in their community that pertained to their interests. This provided them with informative resources and valuable connections.

Months flew by, and soon it was time for college applications. Bradley and Bernadette were prepared due to their future planning strategy. They researched which colleges were best for their respective fields and what scholarships they could apply for. Their proactive steps made the application process smooth, and they were accepted into their dream colleges.

As they stepped into college, they continued their future planning by creating new desires and standards to uphold themselves as they consistently assessed their progress. They interned in their respective fields, gaining hands-on experience and making more connections along the way.

Fast forward a few years, and Bradley and Bernadette both achieved their dreams. Bradley was now working on cutting-edge engineering projects while Bernadette had started her own thriving business. Looking back, they realized that planning and taking proactive steps early in their teenage years was crucial to their success.

Through their friendly yet determined collaboration, Bradley and Bernadette showcased the importance of future planning for teenagers. Taking proactive steps not only helped them achieve their dreams but also made them more confident and prepared individuals. In the same way, young readers should follow Bradley and Bernadette's example, as it is never too early to start planning for your future, create action plans, and build connections. By doing so, they may also find success by turning their dreams into reality.

Shaping Dreams into Reality

As a teenager, you're like an artist with a blank canvas, ready to paint your own unique masterpiece called "your future." You might have dreams of becoming an astronaut, a doctor, a movie star, or a CEO—the possibilities are endless.

You should believe you can paint your future whatever you set your heart and mind to, but you should also look at the most realistic options for you without compromising or selling your capabilities short. However, as exciting as it may seem, planning for your future requires careful consideration, thoughtful decision-making, and a realistic understanding of your strengths, interests, and options.

- Know yourself: The first step in future planning is self-assessment. Identify your strengths, passions, interests, and values. Ask yourself, what do you love doing? What comes naturally to you? What matters most to you in life? Reflecting on these questions will help you discover who you are and what you genuinely desire for your future, making it easier to set achievable desires.

- Identify your areas of interest: Before diving into college research, reflect on your interests, passions, and career aspirations. Are you fascinated by technology and eager to explore computer science? Maybe you have a creative flair and are considering a degree in design or fine arts. Knowing your interests will help narrow down your list of potential colleges and universities.

- Explore different careers: Since the world is full of various professions and industries, learn what you can, about different careers and understand what each one entails. By researching various fields, you'll be able to narrow down your options and select the ones that resonate with your skills and passions.

- Set realistic goals: Building a successful future starts with identifying clear, achievable goals. Consider your interests, strengths, and the amount of work and commitment required for each path. Setting ambitious yet attainable goals will inspire and motivate you to work harder and stay focused on your dreams.

- Obtain essential education and skills: In today's competitive world, it's crucial to have the right education and skills to thrive in your chosen field. High school is just the beginning; often, pursuing higher education—whether that's a college degree, vocational training, or an apprenticeship—will unlock more career opportunities and help you gain essential expertise.

- Develop a strong work ethic: No matter which career you choose; hard work and dedication are significant keys to success. Treat school, internships, or part-time jobs as opportunities to build valuable experience and cultivate a solid work ethic that will help you stand out in your field.

- Learn from mentors: Look for role models within your chosen field, and don't hesitate to reach out to them for advice and guidance. Learning from those who have succeeded before you will provide valuable insights that can help shape your path and make better decisions along the way.

- Adapt to change: Remember that the world is constantly evolving, and so too, should your plans. Be open to revising your plans if you discover new passions or if certain opportunities arise. Staying flexible and adaptable is a valuable trait that will allow you to navigate the uncertainties of life with greater ease and confidence.

- Begin your research early: Don't wait until your final year of high school to start researching colleges and universities. Starting early will give you ample time to explore various options, understand the admission criteria, and identify which institutions might be the best fit for you.

- Use various resources to research colleges and universities: Apart from the Internet, tap into additional sources like school counselors, teachers, family friends, and older siblings or friends who have gone through the college application process. These individuals can provide valuable first-hand knowledge and experiences to help guide you in your research.

- Learn about each institution's strengths and focus areas: As you research various colleges and universities, pay special attention to the fields they are known for, their rankings in those fields, and their resources and opportunities specific to those disciplines. This information will help you understand if a particular institution aligns with your interests and goals.

- Understand admission criteria and acceptance rates: Different colleges and universities have varying admission criteria, which may include standardized test scores, grade point average (GPA), extracurricular involvement, and essays. Make sure to research the specific requirements for each institution you're considering and plan accordingly. Also, take note of acceptance rates, which can help you gauge the competitiveness of each school.

- Attend fairs and open houses: College fairs and open houses can provide valuable insights into campus life, academic programs, and facilities. These events offer the opportunity to speak with current students, faculty, and admissions representatives, who can help answer your questions and provide a better understanding of each institution.

- Visit campuses, if possible: If you have the opportunity, visiting college campuses can help you get a feel for the environment and culture of the institution. You can also talk to students and faculty members, attend classes or events, and assess whether the campus environment aligns with your preferences.

- Research scholarships and financial aid options: Begin researching scholarship opportunities and financial aid programs and applications early on, as deadlines can vary. By being proactive in your search for financial assistance, you increase your chances of obtaining funding for your education.

- Seek support from others: Remember, you don't have to navigate this process alone. Reach out to your support network and collaborate with your peers who might be going through the same experience. By sharing research and advice, you can help each other make informed decisions and prepare for the future.

Planning for your future as a teenager might feel overwhelming, but by taking these steps, you can be better prepared to make informed decisions about your education and career goals. Understanding the resources available to you, conducting thorough research, and utilizing your support network will help set you on the right path for success, and even ahead of your peers.

Top 10 Questions in Choosing a College

Looking at colleges, researching majors, and talking to recruiters can be challenging. Keeping track of all the information you receive and deciphering what's important can be even tougher. Here are a handful of questions to help you get started:

1. What type of academic programs and degree offerings does the college provide? This question will help determine if the college offers the field of study that interests you and whether that particular school offers the degree you are interested in.

2. How successful are students who graduate from this college? It's important to know how successful college graduates have been regarding job placement, further education, and other accomplishments.

3. What is the student-to-faculty ratio? A low student-to-faculty ratio can be beneficial, as it

may result in more individualized attention for students in class settings and during office hours.

4. What is the cost of tuition and fees? You need to know the total cost associated with attending a given school before making your decision.

5. Is financial aid available? If so, what types of aid are offered, and how can they be applied for? Knowing what types of financial assistance are available at different schools can make a major difference in deciding which one to attend.

6. Are there any special programs or activities available to get involved in at this college? It's always nice to have options for activities outside of the classroom, so find out if there are clubs, sports teams, or other organizations you could join while attending this particular school.

7. How easy is it to get around campus and access other areas of town from here? Knowing how accessible transportation options are from campus can help determine how much time you would need to spend traveling back and forth from home or work each day.

8. Does this college offer any internship or co-op opportunities for students? Gaining real-world experience through internships or co-ops can be extremely valuable when it comes time to start looking for jobs after graduation, so find out if

these options exist at the college you're considering attending ahead of time if possible.

9. What do previous students have to say about their experiences at this school? Talking with alumni or current students can provide perspective on what it's really like attending classes there every day rather than just relying on advertising materials put out by the university itself.

10. Are there any housing options near campus that I could consider living in while attending here? Knowing what your housing options are before enrolling in a college can save you a lot of stress down the line, so try doing some research into

nearby apartments or dorms that might suit your needs prior to selecting a school.

Reflection Questions

Have you thought about what you want to be or do when you're an adult? If so, what are some ideas you have?

_____

_____

_____

_____

_____

_____

_____

_____

Do you think it will be tough to venture into this career or college path? If yes, what strategies can you utilize to make the transition easier?

_____

_____

_____

_____

_____

_____

_____

_____

What resources are available to you that can help you make an informed decision about your education and career path?

_____

_____

_____

_____

_____

_____

_____

What support network (friends, family, mentors, etc.) can help you with the college selection/career path process?

What are some questions you have about the colleges you're considering or the career paths you're interested in?

What are some of the pros and cons associated with each college or career path you've considered?

_____

_____

_____

_____

_____

_____

_____

_____

What are you looking for in a college or in further education?

_____

_____

_____

_____

_____

_____

_____

If you are considering skipping further education or putting it off for a little while, what do you plan to do in the meantime? How will you use your time? For instance, will you travel or start your own business?

Conclusion

Congratulations! You have completed *The Ultimate Teen Life Skills* book. I encourage you to reflect on what you've read, what you've learned, and the impact this book may have had on your life.

What have been the biggest takeaways for you? What have been your most valuable lessons? Thank you for taking the time to read through this book. I hope that it was an enjoyable and enlightening experience. It's okay if you don't understand all the information at once. Or maybe some information will apply to you at different stages. As you age, have new and original experiences, and learn new skills, the same concepts may have a different impact on you. You can now use the knowledge that you've gained to find your own solutions and better understand your circumstances.

Reread the chapters, earmark your favorite sections, and use the worksheets to practice and develop your own personal development skills. The journey of personal growth is lifelong. Right now, it may seem like the adults have it all figured out and know exactly what they're doing when they should do it, and how they should do it. But the truth is that even for the most successful adults not everything is a breeze at times. While most grownups have more information, knowledge, and wisdom than you, there are still areas for improvement at any stage of life.

Think about it; you can use your full potential for anything you like to become in the future—from being a rocket scientist or doctor one day to becoming a dancer or even a writer yourself. We all have uncommon knowledge, distinct experiences, and perspectives. We can learn from each other, regardless of age—you have a lot to offer as well.

That's why as a teen, you can have more potential than adults and take advantage of the options available to start your personal development and growth journey. You can use this information to your advantage and make the best out of it. Invest in yourself, invest in learning more, and access the resources that help you improve. You will thank yourself for it later.

Everyone is still learning, growing, and improving their lives with these same life skills because the only way to really become the best version of yourself is through continuous learning and exploration. So don't be afraid to use this book to help you understand the world better and, eventually, become successful adults.

Making mistakes, feeling fear, and experiencing failure are all experiences that every person, from teen to adult, will go through. Without contrast, we wouldn't know what we truly want. However, the difference between the successful and unsuccessful lies in how they respond and use their skills to bounce back faster. As a brief reminder, here are a few major key takeaways for teens looking to improve their self-development skills:

- Understand yourself and your values, beliefs, and thought patterns

- Learn to communicate effectively with others

- Develop emotional intelligence and stress management techniques

- Cultivate resilience and a positive mindset

- Pursue personal growth through learning, exploration, and experimentation

- Take ownership of your choices and actions

Ultimately, the goal is to reach adulthood with the necessary skills and knowledge to live a happy life. With this book, I hope you can see that those difficult moments in life are valuable learning experiences and opportunities to grow and become stronger. But now, you have the tools and skills to take on life with more confidence and resilience.

As I mentioned earlier, all the provided tips and methods in this book have tremendously helped my own family and other teens, that I've had the pleasure of coaching! My goal by writing this book is to reach out and help as many parents and teens as possible, to feel more confident going through this important developmental stage and be successful.

You can also help other parents and teens, simply by leaving a review on how this book has helped you to gain essential life skills. You'll be making it easier for others to also find the information that can make the teen journey more enjoyable by clicking below:

https://www.amazon.com/review

https://www.amazon.ca/review

https://www.amazon.co.uk/review

I hope this has been an enlightening journey for you, one that will help you become a more confident and self-aware individual who knows exactly what kind of life they want to lead. With these new valuable insights, you can learn more about yourself, others, and the world around you. Remember to keep learning, increase your self-awareness, and practice what you learned here today. It's never too late to start! Good luck, and enjoy the journey ahead! Take care.

References

Albano, A. M. (2021, May 20). *Is social media threatening teens' mental health and well-being?* Columbia University Irving Medical Center. https://www.cuimc.columbia.edu/news/social-media-threatening-teens-mental-health-and-well-being

Ben-Joseph, E. P. (2018). *Online safety (for teens).* Kidshealth.org. https://kidshealth.org/en/teens/internet-safety.html

Browne, K. (2015, February 18). *Organize your bedroom: A step-by-step guide for teenagers.* Www.getorganizedwizard.com. https://www.getorganizedwizard.com/blog/2015/02/organize-bedroom-step-step-guide-teenagers/

Center for Parent and Teen Communication. (2019, November 25). *What is consent?* Center for Parent and Teen Communication. https://parentandteen.com/what-is-consent/

Clifton, T. (2022, April 13). *Exercise for teenagers: A complete guide.* Healthline.

https://www.healthline.com/health/fitness/exercise-for-teenagers

D'Amico, P. (2021, July 21). *8 relaxation techniques for teens.* Paradigm Treatment. https://paradigmtreatment.com/relaxation-techniques-teen/

Ehmke, R. (2022, December 6). *How using social media affects teenagers.* Child Mind Institute. https://childmind.org/article/how-using-social-media-affects-teenagers/

Feminine hygiene tips every girl should know. (n.d.). Tampax.co.uk. https://tampax.co.uk/en-gb/period-health/feminine-hygiene-tips/

Floras, K. D. (2020, February 4). *How study breaks help teenagers in the exam preparation, tips to help teenage students take effective study breaks while preparing for exams.* Www.parentcircle.com. https://www.parentcircle.com/how-study-breaks-help-children-in-the-exam-preparation/article

Giving directions in English. (2019, December 1). Www.wallstreetenglish.com. https://www.wallstreetenglish.com/blog/giving-directions-in-english

Guo, Z., & Zhang, Y. (2022). Study on the interactive factors between physical exercise and mental health promotion of teenagers. *Journal of*

Healthcare Engineering, *2022*, e4750133. https://doi.org/10.1155/2022/4750133

Helm, B. (2017). *Friendship.* Stanford.edu. https://plato.stanford.edu/entries/friendship/

Herrity, J. (2019, December 12). *How to write SMART goals (with examples).* Indeed Career Guide. https://www.indeed.com/career-advice/career-development/how-to-write-smart-goals

Hunter, L. (2020, November 20). *5 ways to help your teen build healthy romantic relationships.* Center for Parent and Teen Communication. https://parentandteen.com/healthy-romantic-relationships/

Investment calculator. (n.d.). Bankrate. https://www.bankrate.com/investing/investment-goal-calculator/

Jen. (2020, September 22). *How to organize a teen's bedroom: 9 functional ideas.* Organizenvy. https://organizenvy.com/organize-teens-bedroom/

Kelly, A. (2019, January 16). *Take charge of your health: A guide for teenagers.* National Institute of Diabetes and Digestive and Kidney Diseases. https://www.niddk.nih.gov/health-information/weight-management/take-charge-health-guide-teenagers

Kirkman, V. (2020, February 25). *Using social media responsibly.* Youth First.

https://youthfirstinc.org/using-social-media-responsibly/

Maxabella, B. (2020, June 22). *Frenemies: 8 tips to help kids manage mean friends.* Mumlyfe. https://mumlyfe.com.au/frenemies/

McDonald, T. (2018, May 17). *How peer pressure affects teen development.* Crossroads Health. https://crossroadshealth.org/how-peer-pressure-affects-teen-development/

Miller, C. (2019, February 27). *Just enough for you: About food portions.* National Institute of Diabetes and Digestive and Kidney Diseases. https://www.niddk.nih.gov/health-information/weight-management/just-enough-food-portions

Mind Tools Content Team. (2022). *What is time mangement?* Www.mindtools.com. https://www.mindtools.com/arb6j5a/what-is-time-management

Monroe, J. (2012, December 15). *The effects of teenage hormones on adolescent emotions.* Newport Academy; Newport Academy. https://www.newportacademy.com/resources/empowering-teens/teenage-hormones-and-sexuality/

Morin, A. (n.d.). *7 ways to help teens and tweens gain self-awareness.* Www.understood.org. https://www.understood.org/en/articles/7-

ways-to-help-teens-and-tweens-gain-self-awareness

Morin, A. (2015, February 16). *Are my teen's mood swings normal?* Verywell Family; Verywellfamily. https://www.verywellfamily.com/are-my-teens-mood-swings-normal-2611240

Oakes, T. (2017, October 7). *6 tips on communicating with others.* ELearning Industry; eLearning Industry. https://elearningindustry.com/communicating-with-others-6-tips

Pierce, R. (2020, November 19). *Teaching diverse learners about banking.* Lifeskillsadvocate.com. https://lifeskillsadvocate.com/blog/teaching-diverse-learners-about-banking/

Raising Children Network. (2017, December 11). *Brain development in pre-teens and teenagers.* Raising Children Network. https://raisingchildren.net.au/pre-teens/development/understanding-your-pre-teen/brain-development-teens

Ranscombe, S. (2018, August 15). *Study finds that make-up ages you - but only up to a certain point.* Harper's BAZAAR. https://www.harpersbazaar.com/uk/beauty/make-up-nails/a22734615/study-finds-that-make-up-ages-you-but-only-up-to-a-certain-point/

Rawat, Y. (2021, September 24). *How social media negatively affects our critical thinking.* The Phoenix.

https://fhsphoenix.org/how-social-media-negatively-affects-our-critical-thinking/

Reed, B. (2022, July 10). *How social media could be harming your child's attention span.* Www.cbsnews.com. https://www.cbsnews.com/pittsburgh/news/how-social-media-could-be-harming-your-childs-attention-span/

Saraswat, K. (2014, June 12). *10 hygiene tips every guy must follow!* TheHealthSite. https://www.thehealthsite.com/beauty/10-hygiene-tips-every-guy-must-follow-169105/

Schwarz, N. (n.d.). *15 tips to build self esteem and confidence in teens.* Big Life Journal. https://biglifejournal.com/blogs/blog/build-self-esteem-confidence-teens

Schwarz, N. (2017). *How to teach growth mindset to teens.* Big Life Journal. https://biglifejournal.com/blogs/blog/teaching-teens-growth-mindset

Securly. (2018, October 4). *The 10 types of cyberbullying.* Blog. https://blog.securly.com/10/04/2018/the-10-types-of-cyberbullying/

Shenfield, T. (2017, October 16). *How to communicate with your teen through active listening.* Child Psychology Resources by Dr. Tali Shenfield.

https://www.psy-ed.com/wpblog/communicate-with-teen/

Sippl, A. (2021, October 7). *Empowering teens: 25 life skills they need to know + PDF checklist.* Lifeskillsadvocate.com. https://lifeskillsadvocate.com/blog/25-daily-living-skills-every-teen-should-know/

Spencer, E. (2018, October 8). *Teenage mood swings: 7 tips.* Your Teen Magazine. https://yourteenmag.com/family-life/communication/teenage-mood-swings

Staff Blogs. (n.d.). *25 questions to ask yourself when choosing a college.* https://wealthyhabits.org/25-questions-to-ask-yourself-when-choosing-a-college/

Stern, J., & Samson, R. (2021, August 3). *How to build teens' empathy.* Www.psychologytoday.com. https://www.psychologytoday.com/us/blog/the-heart-and-science-attachment/202108/how-build-teens-empathy

Thrive Training and Consulting. (2021, November 11). *Tips for teens: Building healthy communication skills.* Thrive Training Consulting. https://www.thrivetrainingconsulting.com/tips-for-teens-building-healthy-communication-skills/

Understanding social media use and balance. (n.d.). The Jed Foundation.

https://jedfoundation.org/resource/understanding-social-media-use-and-balance/

Vogels, E. (2022, December 15). *Teens and cyberbullying 2022*. Pew Research Center. https://www.pewresearch.org/internet/2022/12/15/teens-and-cyberbullying-2022/

Walsh, D. (2012, November 13). *Teenage dating: Romance and the brain*. Spark & Stitch Institute. https://sparkandstitchinstitute.com/teenage-dating-romance-and-the-brain/

Watkins, L. (2017, February 7). *Teens and social media: The highlight reel effect*. LearningWorks for Kids. https://learningworksforkids.com/2017/02/teens-and-social-media-the-highlight-reel-effect/

Weinstein, T. (2022, November 2). *Teenage love and relationships: What parents can expect*. Newport Academy. https://www.newportacademy.com/resources/empowering-teens/teenage-love/

Witmer, D. (2021, January 31). *6 ways parents can help their teens deal with mood swings*. Verywell Family. https://www.verywellfamily.com/help-your-teen-control-mood-swings-2610554

Your Teen Magazine. (2019, February 5). *"mom, i'm bored!" 100 activities antsy teens can do without screens*. Your Teen Magazine. https://yourteenmag.com/family-life/communication/100-things-teenagers-can-do-without-screens

Yourtherapysource. (2022, August 11). *SMART goals for teens*. Your Therapy Source. https://www.yourtherapysource.com/blog1/2022/08/11/smart-goals-for-teens-3/

Made in the USA
Middletown, DE
11 June 2024